BLACK BELT
SUDOKU™

Michael Rios

Sterling Publishing Co., Inc.
New York

CONTENTS

Introduction

3

Puzzles

5

Answers

155

8   10   9

Martial Arts Sudoku and Black Belt Sudoku
are trademarks of Sterling Publishing Co., Inc.

Published by Sterling Publishing Co., Inc.
387 Park Avenue South, New York, NY 10016
© 2005 by Michael Rios
Distributed in Canada by Sterling Publishing
c/o Canadian Manda Group, 165 Dufferin Street,
Toronto, Ontario, Canada M6K 3H6
Distributed in the United Kingdom by GMC Distribution Services,
Castle Place, 166 High Street, Lewes, East Sussex, England BN7 1XU
Distributed in Australia by Capricorn Link (Australia) Pty. Ltd.
P.O. Box 704, Windsor, NSW 2756, Australia

Sterling ISBN-13: 978-1-4027-3598-1
ISBN-10: 1-4027-3598-7

For information about custom editions, special sales, premium and
corporate purchases, please contact Sterling Special Sales
Department at 800-805-5489 or specialsales@sterlingpub.com.

INTRODUCTION

To solve sudoku puzzles, all you need to know is this one simple rule:

Fill in the boxes so that each of the nine rows, each of the nine columns, and each of the nine 3×3 sections contain all the numbers from 1 to 9.

And that's all there is to it! Using these simple rules, let's see how far we get on this sample puzzle at right. (The letters at the top and left edges of the puzzle are for reference only; you won't see them in the regular puzzles.)

	A	B	C	D	E	F	G	H	I
J									
K					2		1	8	4
L	9		5		7		2		6
M	1		4	3	9	2		7	
N				7		6			
O		7		1	4	8	9		2
P	3		2		6		8		5
Q	8	4	9		3				
R									

The first number that can be filled in is an obvious one: box EN is the only blank box in the center 3×3 section, and all the digits 1 through 9 are represented except for 5. EN must be 5.

The next box is a little trickier to discover. Consider the upper left 3×3 section of the puzzle. Where can a 4 go? It can't go in AK, BK, or CK because row K already has a 4 at IK. It can't go in BJ or BL because column B already has a 4 at BQ. It can't go in CJ because column C already has a 4 at CM. So it must go in AJ.

Another box in that same section that can now be filled is BJ. A 2 can't go in AK, BK, or CK due to the 2 at EK. The 2 at GL rules out a 2 at BL. And the 2 at CP means that a 2 can't go in CJ. So BJ must contain the 2. It is worth noting that this 2 couldn't have been placed without the 4 at AJ in place. Many of the puzzles rely on this type of steppingstone behavior.

We now have a grid as shown.

Let's examine column A. There are four blank boxes in column A; in which blank box must the 2 be placed? It can't be AK because of the 2 in EK (and the 2 in BJ). It can't be AO because of the 2 in IO. It can't be AR because of the 2 in CP. Thus, it must be AN that has the 2.

	A	B	C	D	E	F	G	H	I
J	4	2							
K					2		1	8	4
L	9		5		7		2		6
M	1		4	3	9	2		7	
N				7	5	6			
O		7		1	4	8	9		2
P	3		2		6		8		5
Q	8	4	9		3				
R									

By the 9's in AL, EM, and CQ, box BN must be 9. Do you see how?

We can now determine the value for box IM. Looking at row M and then column I, we find all the digits 1 through 9 are represented but 8. IM must be 8.

This brief example of some of the techniques leaves us with the grid at right.

You should now be able to use what you learned to fill in CN followed by BL, then HL followed by DL and FL.

As you keep going through this puzzle, you'll find it gets easier as you fill in more. And as you keep working through the puzzles in this book, you'll find it gets easier and more fun each time. The final answer is shown below.

This book consists of 300 puzzles of super-tough level of difficulty.

—Michael Rios

	A	B	C	D	E	F	G	H	I
J	4	2							
K					2		1	8	4
L	9		5		7		2		6
M	1		4	3	9	2		7	8
N	2	9		7	5	6			
O		7		1	4	8	9		2
P	3		2		6		8		5
Q	8	4	9		3				
R									

	A	B	C	D	E	F	G	H	I
J	4	2	1	6	8	3	5	9	7
K	7	3	6	5	2	9	1	8	4
L	9	8	5	4	7	1	2	3	6
M	1	5	4	3	9	2	6	7	8
N	2	9	8	7	5	6	4	1	3
O	6	7	3	1	4	8	9	5	2
P	3	1	2	9	6	7	8	4	5
Q	8	4	9	2	3	5	7	6	1
R	5	6	7	8	1	4	3	2	9

1

		9						
4					5	1		
2	6	3				9		
				8	9			3
		1		6		2		
5			1	4				
		2				5	9	8
		8	9					6
						4		

2

							3	9
5	8							
2			1			5	6	
		6	5		4		2	
4								5
	7		3		6	8		
	9	8			3			6
							4	1
7	6							

3

		9						
2		7	9				3	5
	3		2					
						8	1	4
	1			3			2	
8	6	4						
					5		9	
3	4				6	1		2
						4		

4

							4	3
							6	
2	8			1		5	9	
		3	4	7		6		
			9		1			
		1		5	6	3		
	1	8		9			7	2
	9							
6	5							

5

9	8		7			6		
7	3					5	1	
			6					2
			4					8
		5				4		
4					3			
8				2				
	5	1					3	6
		9			1		5	7

6

							2	1
				9	5			6
						5		4
		5			9	4		8
7				4				5
6		2	7			3		
3		9						
2			8	7				
5	6							

Puzzle 7:

						7	1	
	2			4	9			8
6			8				9	
			2	3				
	8		9		1		6	
				7	8			
	9				4			1
8			3	6			5	
	3	7						

Puzzle 8:

				2				
	1	5						
	2		3	9		8		
	7					3	6	9
6			8		4			1
2	5	1					7	
		4		6	7		1	
						2	5	
				4				

Puzzle 9

	6				8		2	
	7			1				
	4		9		2		6	
			1					3
9				5				8
4					6			
	8		5		1		7	
				3			1	
	5		2				3	

Puzzle 10

			2	6	4			
						5		4
4	2			1				
		6	5				8	
3	8						1	9
	9				3	6		
				4			6	8
7		9						
			1	2	6			

Puzzle 11

		8						6
					9	1		
			1			9	5	8
	2	4		3				
	8		6		1		9	
				7		4	6	
3	4	1			2			
		6	5					
9						3		

Puzzle 12

			7	1		5		9
								1
8			2					
1	7				4	8		
		5		9		6		
		4	6				5	2
					5			4
4								
6		2		8	3			

	1				2			
							4	
		3	9	8		7		
3			7					5
8		7		5		1		6
6					1			2
		2		4	7	3		
	5							
			2				8	

	5			2		7		1
		9			3	8		
				7		5		4
	6					9	1	
	2	4					6	
6		7		1				
		5	4			6		
8		3		5			4	

15

1								8
		2		1	3			6
	9				2		1	
						5	7	
3		8				2		9
	4	6						
	3		1				4	
5			6	4		3		
9								2

16

		5		2				6
			1					4
		7		6		5		
4								2
	6		3	4	9		8	
8								7
		9		1		6		
1					8			
3				7		8		

	4							
9			6	8		5		
1			2			4	8	
	8			7			2	
	7			1			9	
	5	3			6			7
		8		5	3			9
							4	

				3		8	4	1
7			6		5			
8				4	2		7	
		4		7		6		
	1		3	6				2
			8		7			9
9	3	8		2				

Puzzle 19:

		4				9		1
3			7		9			
7								3
		8	2			3		5
				6				
9		5			3	2		
4								8
			1		5			6
8		9				7		

Puzzle 20:

				9	1			8
		4					9	2
			6				1	4
6		5						1
			3		5			
7						2		5
3	6				7			
5	2					7		
1			9	5				

Puzzle 2/1

3		6	9			1		
	5	1					6	
					7		2	
			8					9
	8			5			4	
4					1			
	2		6					
	4					5	1	
		8			9	7		2

Puzzle 2/2

8							7	4
6				2	7	1		
	4					5		
					2			6
	2		5		8		9	
3			7					
		8					4	
		7	6	5				1
1	9							7

2/3

6							1	
		7			1			
3				4	5			9
7				9		8	3	
			2		8			
	5	9		3				1
4			7	2				3
			8			6		
	3							8

2/4

				5		4	1	
	7	9						
						8		3
	6				3			8
3		8	4		7	2		6
5			9				7	
8		6						
						6	8	
	2	1		8				

			5			7	6	9
3					4	5		
	8			1				4
	5						1	
				3				
	6						4	
2				6			9	
		7	1					8
6	4	9			7			

8			5	9	2			
9			1	7		3		
						1		
		7			8			
	3	5				6	1	
			3			9		
		6						
		8		5	1			7
			6	8	4			5

		6			3			
	8							
				2		1	3	9
6				7	1		5	8
	4						7	
1	9		5	4				2
8	1	4		6				
							4	
			4			2		

5			7		9			
7	3						8	
		1		5				
9			2		1			
8		3				2		7
			8		7			1
				6		7		
	4						1	9
			5		8			4

	8							9
	3			6	1			
		9			5	7	2	
			5			4		3
			7		3			
3		4			9			
	1	7	8			3		
			4	9			6	
5							4	

4			2				8	
	6					1		
		5		9				
6							1	9
1		3	5		2	6		7
5	4							8
				7		2		
		9					5	
	3				9			6

Puzzle 3-1:

	6	8						9
5			4	7				6
		5		1	7	2		
		7	9		3	5		
		1	6	2		8		
4				6	1			3
2						9	4	

Puzzle 3-2:

				6			2	5
						9		6
			9	1	8			7
2		7						
		3		5		6		
						4		3
8			5	2	4			
1		5						
4	6			8				

					1		8	5
					2	9	3	
6				4			7	
			2	5			1	
		7				2		
	9			6	3			
	8			2				1
	3	9	7					
2	6		4					

			8	4		3		7
					3	9		
		1					4	6
		6	9				3	
	1				7	8		
8	5					2		
		3	4					
7		4		6	9			

Puzzle 3/5:

	6		3	8				
	9	8	6			5		
								2
4	7	1		9				
			1		7			
				4		1	3	7
6								
		5			6	7	1	
				3	9		4	

Puzzle 3/6:

			2			5	4	7
		2	5			3		6
					9			2
					5		8	
		8				9		
	7		8					
8			4					
7		6			3	2		
5	4	1			6			

						8	4	1
5								
		4		6	9	2		
				5		9		
7		1	8		4	5		3
		8		7				
		7	3	4		1		
								7
3	2	6						

		7			6	5		9
	6		9					
		3	4					
7			5					3
6	1						4	2
8					2			1
					1	8		
					8		7	
3		9	7			2		

		3	4	9			5	
		7						2
4								
8		9	7	2			1	
		1				3		
	3			6	1	5		7
								1
9						2		
	8			1	2	6		

		9	7					3
			1	8	6			
	2	6		9			4	
	1					2	8	
	3	8					9	
	7			1		3	2	
			9	6	2			
8					5	6		

4-1

	2					4	5	
5				4	1		3	
		7					2	
			7		9		1	
1								9
	8		4		6			
	9					6		
	1		6	2				5
	4	3					8	

4-2

								1
	8	9						7
	2		3	4	5			
		7	9					
	4		8	6	2		5	
					7	8		
			6	3	8		4	
6						9	8	
2								

6		1		2	4			7
	3		6					
7		4						
	8						5	6
				8				
3	9						1	
						1		2
					3		9	
2			7	6		8		5

	4				6		2	8
	9		5		3			
				2				
8				1			6	7
		7				1		
1	2			5				9
				7				
			2		9		8	
6	5		4				1	

					2	1	7	
	5	4			8	6		
	8			3		9		
6					5			
				1				
			3					4
		1		8			2	
		2	6			5	9	
	3	6	7					

6				5			3	
	8		9	2		5		
	2					4	7	
						7		
3			7		1			8
		8						
	9	1					8	
		4		6	2		1	
	6			4				7

4/7

				8		5		
1		7	5					
		2				3		7
8			7				6	4
		4				9		
9	3				8			2
5		9				4		
				7		6		9
		1		6				

4/8

1		4	2				8	
	2	9				5		
					6			9
3			8			7		
		2				1		
		5			1			6
2			3					
		6				4	9	
	5				7	8		2

			6			1		
9			7			5		8
		1	9					
6						8		
2	9			5			3	7
		4						9
					6	7		
8		7			1			3
		5			9			

7		1	5		6			
						2	7	4
3	9							
						5	9	8
			1		8			
8	7	6						
							5	2
6	5	9						
			7		9	4		3

	9				2			
	1		7		3	4		
	2			8				
		8		4	1	9		
	4						7	
		2	8	6		5		
				9			8	
		7	3		8		1	
			4				3	

	5							1
		4				3	2	
		9	6		4			
	3		8			2	6	9
6	2	1			7		5	
			3		5	4		
	7	3				5		
1							9	

Puzzle 5 / 3

	8		6					3
4	3		8	7				
			3		4			
						1	4	6
	4						8	
5	2	8						
		7		1				
			4	3			1	9
6					5		7	

Puzzle 5 / 4

							3	
	3	7	1	6			8	
	2		7					
	4	1						6
		6		1		7		
9						1	2	
					2		1	
	9			3	7	4	5	
	8							

6				3				
5	9				4			
			2		5			
9				6			7	
8		4		9		6		5
	1			8				2
			7		9			
			1				4	8
				5				6

	7	2		3				
9	6							
	5		1		7			4
			9	7				
2				1				8
				5	6			
6			4		2		8	
							6	5
				6		1	2	

5 7

		8	4	3	9		2	
7			5			4	9	1
							5	
	8		6		2		3	
	4							
9	2	6			5			8
	1		7	9	3	5		

5 8

7	4	8		2	5			
2					4			
6				3		9		
		9	8				5	
	5				2	3		
		6		8				1
			4					3
			5	1		8	4	7

2						9		7
						4		
					7		2	1
	2	6		7		1		
	5			2			4	
		8		6		7	3	
4	3		5					
		7						
1		2						6

1			7					
								4
		5	2	3			8	9
						1	5	7
2								6
3	7	9						
5	4			1	6	9		
8								
					9			8

Puzzle 6/1

1		7						
			4			7		8
	9	3						6
			5	6				4
2	6						7	3
5				1	2			
9						2	6	
3		5			1			
						3		5

Puzzle 6/2

	2					6		
6	8			4			5	
4		5		9				
	6	4						
3			7		8			6
						9	7	
				1		2		4
	9			2			8	7
		8					9	

6
3

				7	2			4
	9		1	3				
	8		6					5
4		1					3	
	5					4		7
6					9		7	
				1	8		2	
7			2	5				

6
4

		2	1				5	6
	3	1			8	7	4	
			5				1	
7								
			4		1			
								2
	7				3			
	4	6	2			3	9	
3	2				9	4		

1					2	3		
	7		1		8			
			4			2	8	
						8	6	
		4				5		
	9	8						
	2	9			1			
			9		7		2	
		5	3					7

2						8	3	
5		8	4					
				6	2			1
				9		1		
7		4				9		6
		2		4				
3			5	8				
					1	3		8
	2	7						9

1					3			
					5		2	3
	7						9	
		6			8		5	2
8				5				1
2	9		3			6		
	3						7	
9	6		4					
			2					8

	6	5	9	3				
						3		
7	2							
					2	7		5
3		8		9		4		2
2		9	6					
							8	7
		1						
				4	3	9	1	

7/1

5		6		4	1		9	
			6					
	9	8	3					5
			7				2	
		5				1		
	3				4			
9					5	3	4	
					8			
	4		2	3		7		9

7/2

	5	4	1					6
		2						
8		1			3			
2				3				8
	9			5			3	
7				4				5
			3			5		2
						7		
4					7	3	1	

7	9		6					8
8				5			7	
	1		3				6	
9	6		7					
					4		1	5
	3				1		2	
	8			4				7
5					6		9	3

6			8	4	7		9	
8		5			1		2	
	4		3	1				9
7				6	8		4	
	5		1			7		3
	8		7	3	5			1

							2	6
				1	2			
1	6			5		9	3	
					1	5		9
9								3
7		1	8					
	9	3		8			6	1
			4	3				
6	5							

3								
6		2	5		1			
1			9	4	6			
9		5	8			7		
		8			4	6		9
			2	6	5			3
			4		3	2		5
								7

		4						2
8						4		5
	6		4		3			
				2		6		3
		9	5		8	7		
4		1		6				
			8		7		2	
1		8						7
7						1		

			6			4		
3	2					6		
			7		2	9		
	5			2			3	
			5	9	1			
	6			7			1	
		5	4		3			
		2					8	4
		4			9			

					9	3		6
		3				7		9
			8		6			5
9		1	3					
		2				8		
				2	1			3
1			7		5			
6		4				9		
3		8	1					

		8			7	6		9
	7		5		8		4	
4							8	
			1					3
2								6
6					5			
	5							2
	3		7		4		9	
1		9	3			4		

					2	8	1	
3			6		7		9	
8								5
9							5	
	6		5		1		8	
	8							9
4								7
	9		7		5			2
	1	7	2					

	5							
	9		7	1		4		
		4	2			9		
					8	3		9
	1		4		2		6	
3		7	1					
		1			6	5		
		6		2	1		8	
							3	

	1		9					
								7
	8	9	2					3
6					7	9		4
	4	5				7	8	
9		1	8					6
3					5	4	2	
8								
					9		6	

	5	4	9			7		
6							5	
			6				1	8
			8	5				7
5								1
7				6	3			
1	2				7			
	4							3
		9			1	4	7	

8/5

				8		5		3
		1	4		9	6		
			2					7
	9						8	
	6		9		5		1	
	7						6	
5				9				
		3	6		1	8		
4		7		5				

8/6

			9					7
7		5			8		3	
4			6		1			
3					2			
6	5						9	2
			3					4
			8		6			3
	1		4			8		6
5					9			

1					6	2		7
7				4				5
		8		3	5		1	
			2					
	9						6	
					3			
	2		4	9		5		
8				2				4
9		6	3					8

		7		5			8	9
		9		1	6		4	
						6	1	
			9		7			
8								3
			1		4			
	9	8						
	2		8	4		1		
3	5			7		2		

		4	7	1	9			8
5					4	9		
2	8							
9							4	
		2				3		
	1							7
							2	9
		7	8					3
6			4	9	5	7		

	9	6					7	
2								9
		7	5	3			6	
							5	3
			4	5	1			
6	1							
	4			8	2	9		
8								2
	7					5	3	

5	1				2	7		
	4	3		9				
		7	6				1	
1		2						
			3		8			
						5		8
	3				7	2		
				3		8	7	
		5	4				9	3

	6		2		4			
		3		9				5
	8				3		7	2
	4	7						
			8		9			
						6	9	
5	9		6				3	
1				8		5		
			5		2		8	

			3	2				
	1						6	4
6	7					3		
	4				1	8	9	
				5				
	8	7	6				5	
		9					8	7
8	2						1	
				6	3			

9			6			3		
	5	7		2			6	
		2						9
6	7	8	4					
					5	4	1	6
8						2		
	3			1		6	4	
		9			4			5

	1	5				3		
3								6
					3		4	
	6			5		1		
8		4		7		9		5
		9		6			3	
	4		5					
2								8
		3				2	1	

								6
		7	5		3		1	
			1				2	7
		2					3	8
6	8						7	5
4	5					6		
2	7				6			
	3		4		8	1		
5								

97

	4			3	5			
					7			
7	6				9	4		2
5	3	1					6	
	8					9	4	7
6		9	2				5	3
			7					
			5	1			9	

98

5					1		2	
1	8		4		6	5		
6		4		9	2			5
2			8	1		6		3
		7	3		8		1	6
	4		5					9

		7			1			
8	5	4	6					
	6	9	8					
6					5		2	
	8						6	
	3		9					1
				8	7	9		
				2	4	1	3	
			7		8			

				8		6		
4		7				3	5	
				2	3			
6			3	4			2	
		1				4		
	5			6	1			3
			6	5				
	7	2				8		6
		8		9				

101

					4	5	1	7
					7			9
6				9			2	
			7	2				
2		3				4		1
			3	5				
	9			4				6
5			7					
8	1	2	6					

102

2	4							
			7	2				
		6	5			9	3	
	5			3		2	4	
		7				3		
	1	9		4			7	
	3	5			1	6		
				5	9			
							2	9

6	4		1			9		2
					9	3		
	8				3		6	
		2	8				1	
	9			1		8		
	5		4				8	
		7	6					
1		4			7		5	6

5			2		3			
6		9	8				3	
		2				4		
	6	5			9		7	
	7		6			1	4	
		8				7		
	4				8	9		2
			1		2			3

	8		5				3	
				8				
	7	1		3	9			
5		3			1			9
		7				5		
4			2			7		8
			1	4		9	5	
				9				
	4				8		6	

							4	
	8		6			3	9	2
		3	8					5
	5	2				8		
			9		3			
		6				5	1	
8					1	6		
7	2	9			6		8	
	4							

5	8		3	1				7
		7			8	2		
		6						1
	4	5		6				
			5			9	3	
1					6			
		6	8			7		
2				3	7		4	8

			8			3	2	
					2			7
	5	6						
		7	3				4	9
	8		4		7		5	
4	2				6	1		
						6	1	
3			6					
	7	5			9			

4				7				
	5		4		3	1		
		3	2				4	6
3								
5	7						8	2
								4
9	6				4	8		
		7	3		5		2	
			2					1

3	7					1		
5			6	3				
		2						7
	3	6	2			5		
1								8
		4			8	6	2	
4						3		
				6	4			1
		8					6	9

8	2			1	3	5		
					6			
	4					2		9
6				5		8		
				7				
		3		6				4
5		4					3	
			2					
		1	6	3			4	7

3			1			5		
					4			
2				5		3		
6	8		4					
	9		2	3	5		8	
					8		1	7
		8		6				5
			9					
		7			3			4

	7	3	9			8	2	
		4				3		
					1		5	
							1	6
	3		2		4		8	
5	2							
	4		8					
		2				7		
	9	7			5	1	4	

					4		6	
9						4		8
	3		6				5	
			1			9	4	
1		9				6		3
	5	7			6			
	6				7		8	
4		5						2
	8		3					

			7					
7		1			6		2	
6	2					8		4
8		7	9					5
3					5	4		1
9		5					3	8
	6		3			1		2
					1			

	9	7	3					4
		2		4		1		5
	7		4			8		
			9	5	3			
		5			1		3	
9		1		7		5		
8					6	4	7	

	6		8				4	5
8	5	7						2
2							7	
	3				1			
			2		7			
			4				6	
	2							6
5						2	1	4
1	8				9		3	

		9			2		1	
				8	5	6		
			3				2	4
					4			7
4				6				5
5			8					
2	5				9			
		8	6	5				
	3		7			1		

Puzzle 119

						4	6	
8		5			3		9	1
6					7			
		1					2	9
				8				
9	2					5		
			5					8
4	5		6			3		7
	3	2						

Puzzle 120

	8				6			9
1	5							
3		7	5			4		
	9						4	
		5	7		2	9		
	1						2	
		4			3	8		7
							6	4
5			6				1	

1 2 1

7	8	3			9			5
			6			8		
	2							
		6		7			4	
2			8		3			9
	5			4		7		
							6	
		9			7			
4			3			1	5	8

1 2 2

	4							
	6	8	3	9		7		
7		1					9	
				4	2			1
			6		5			
5			9	3				
	1					8		2
		6		5	8	9	4	
							5	

				2			3	4
1	3				6	8		
	9							
		6			9	7		
	4	5				1	2	
		9	8			4		
							8	
		3	5				1	6
5	2			6				

			5	8			7	2
							9	
	6	1			2	4		
		3		5		7		
				1				
		2		4		3		
		9	3			6	2	
	8							
2	1			6	8			

5						9		
	6	2						
4		1		6	5			
	2			4		5		9
	7						8	
1		8		3			6	
			6	1		3		5
						6	7	
		7						1

4		1		6				8
				2				
	3	6	9					
2		9	7				5	
		4				9		
	8				3	7		6
					5	1	3	
				3				
8				1		6		2

			9	6	1			4
							3	
		2		5			7	
9			6			4	5	
3								1
	6	4			2			9
	7			8		3		
	4							
6			2	3	4			

9			3		4		6	
				7				5
		4			6	9	1	
				2				1
		3				6		
5				8				
	4	6	8			3		
2				3				
	8		4		5			2

	5			4				
		7		3			9	1
	3	6	2					
			9		8		7	
		5				6		
	6		1		2			
					5	3	8	
1	4			2		7		
				9			2	

						3		6
			3		2			
			4	8			7	1
1		6						
7	4	3				6	9	8
						2		4
5	7			1	9			
			8		6			
6		8						

Puzzle 131

6	8	4	1					
2							6	9
					5			
9			8					
5	6						9	7
					2			1
			3					
1	5							6
					8	2	4	3

Puzzle 132

	7		5					
2		8		6				5
						2		1
	8			7			3	
		9	8		4	6		
	5			1			2	
9		7						
1				5		9		4
					9		1	

Puzzle 133

	1			3		9		6
	6			1				
	9					4		
9					3	7		
			4		2			
		4	5					3
		7					6	
				2			5	
5		3		8			2	

Puzzle 134

	8					4		2
		5	2			8	1	
1			5				7	
				1	4			
			6		5			
			8	9				
	2				3			8
	4	9			2	7		
7		1					4	

	8			9	4			
2					5	8		7
		7	2					
9						1	6	
			4		3			
	7	8						2
					9	5		
7		1	8					4
			3	6			2	

			2		1			
				6	7			1
6	7		9	4				
9			3			4		
	2						7	
		3			6			5
				3	8		1	2
7			4	1				
			6		2			

								5
	3	4		1		7		
		8	7	9				
		1	5					8
8			4		6			2
6					2	5		
			5	3	1			
		6	2			9	7	
9								

9		1		4			7	
4					3			
	3	8					5	
1		9	8					
	5						6	
					1	3		9
	6					1	9	
			2					6
	1			8		4		2

			2			9		7
			8			5		
	5		3	6			1	
	2	4			6	8		
		9	7			1	3	
	3			8	1		9	
		7			9			
4		8			2			

2	3		4					
			6				3	
6			7			4	1	
	5		3					1
	2						4	
1					9		7	
	8	4			3			5
	7				1			
					4		9	3

141

				4	9		2	
			8		3			1
								9
	1	4				9		
		9	6	2	5	4		
		2				8	3	
6								
8			1		7			
	3		9	6				

142

6			3			4		7
			4		8			
		8	9			1		
3	8					6		
		4				9		
		2					3	5
		9			1	3		
			7		3			
5		1			4			9

143

			4				5	8
1	2			8		6		
						7	1	
			5			4		
4		9				2		6
		2			9			
	6	3						
		8		1			3	9
9	4				5			

144

	5	7	3			4		1
4								
		9						8
		1		8				6
	3			2			7	
5				9		2		
6						8		
								4
7		4			8	5	2	

	7					8		
2				4		9	5	
1	4		3		5			
					2			
		9		1		6		
			6					
			4		3		2	6
	5	6		7				4
		7					8	

7	8					1		
	2							5
	1	4		8				9
			8					2
		8		4		6		
5					3			
8				6		7	2	
4							3	
		2					5	8

147

	9			7		1	6	8
		5		8	6			
2	6							
	2		7					
		9				5		
					5		8	
							1	3
			9	3		4		
1	4	3		6			2	

148

			9					6
		8				3		5
	2	4	8					
4	1	7			9			
5								9
			5			4	6	7
					7	8	1	
6		1				9		
7					8			

	4		5	7	2		3	
	6	1			8			
							7	9
	9		3	5	7		8	
8	7							
			9			6	5	
	2		1	3	5		4	

		4		2			7	
3						1	5	
9				5	1			
					9	4		
			2	1	5			
		1	8					
			1	9				2
	7	3						8
	1			4		3		

	3				7			
5		8	1					
							1	9
7	9			8		3		
		6	5		9	8		
		3		6			4	5
4	8							
					2	4		8
			9				7	

	6						4	7
8							9	
		9	6					
		3		1				5
		7	8	6	5	4		
2				4		9		
					9	1		
	1							6
5	8						3	

		6		3	9			
2	9	8	7					
		4	1					
	7				8			9
			3		5			
1			9				8	
					4	1		
					1	5	6	2
			6	7		4		

		9	1			5		
6				5			8	7
				9	8			
9	6				3			1
3			4				5	9
			2	6				
2	5			8				4
		1			9	2		

2			9					
6			5					
			3			1	2	4
	9		8					2
	3			4			7	
5					6		4	
4	2	5			3			
					5			8
					1			7

	8			7		1		5
2		6	4				3	
		3			1			
	6					8		
7								3
		8					4	
			5			6		
	9				8	7		1
4		7		1			5	

8					6			
5			8	1				
6				3			9	8
			7				5	
	4			8			6	
	2				9			
9	1			6				3
				2	1			9
			5					1

		5			4			
	6	1			2		4	5
8					3			
	7			8		9		
			3		1			
		8		5			1	
			1					4
6	4		9			7	8	
			2			5		

	5			9				
4				5	1			
9		3	7					
	1		6				9	
2		4				8		7
	3				9		2	
					7	4		8
			3	1				5
				6			1	

	7		9		5		1	
				1				
	2	4	3			5		
5							2	6
				2				
4	9							3
		1			6	7	5	
				4				
	4		2		1		8	

	3				7	1	4	
9	6						2	5
				4				
2				1			9	
3								8
	7			2				1
				5				
8	1						5	2
	5	9	1				3	

	8							
7	9	3			1			
		2	6	7				
2	5			8	9			
	4						5	
			1	5			6	3
				4	2	6		
			8			7	3	2
							9	

	6							2
				5	9	1		
		1					3	4
5	8		9			3		
			7		6			
		9			1		8	6
4	1					5		
		3	2	7				
8							6	

9						6	8	
		8			6	1		
	3							4
					2	7		6
1				5				8
8		9	6					
5							9	
		4	8			2		
	2	7						3

1 6 5

5	7				8			
3		1				8		
9				7		2		
		4	5			3	6	
	3	7			2	9		
		2		4				8
		3				5		2
			8				1	7

1 6 6

3			9	6	2			8
		4		7				
						1	6	
	8	3						
		5	1		9	4		
						2	3	
	2	9						
				9		5		
1			6	5	7			3

Puzzle 167:

						4		3
			1				9	
	1		3			6		
5			2	6		7	3	
	7						2	
	6	2		1	5			4
		1			4		7	
	2				8			
4		8						

Puzzle 168:

						8		
6		2	5					
3	8			7				4
	7				6			9
	9		8		1		2	
4			3				6	
1				3			9	2
					4	3		1
		4						

				1		8	7	
	6	5				4		9
		3	4					1
				8	3			
		6				7		
			1	4				
6					4	2		
7		8				9	3	
	4	1		5				

		9	5					7
8	3		4					
	1			6	8			
	5					8		6
	8						7	
4		1					3	
			8	9			4	
					5		9	8
6					1	2		

			7			2		8
	4	8	5					3
		9		6				5
			8					
		7	9		1	8		
					3			
9				2		3		
5					4	6	1	
6		4			5			

9						7		8
			3				1	
				7	1	6		2
					6	5		3
2								6
4		3	5					
3		8	6	2				
	2				4			
6		4						9

	3		4	1				
					8			
		4	7	3				6
1	6				3		7	
		9				1		
	5		2				8	3
7				9	5	8		
			3					
				2	7		5	

2		8						
1	6		8				5	
		9					2	8
	5		1		9			
7								3
			7		2		6	
6	9					4		
	2				4		8	7
						6		1

1				4				5
9			7					8
			2	1	4			
	2		4					3
		6				8		
3					6		1	
		9	8	3				
5					9			1
4				7				9

	3		7					4
	5			6				9
			1				7	
		7		1		8	2	6
3	9	8		4		7		
	8				4			
4				5			6	
1					2		5	

177

			8					7
					3			4
5			9				3	1
		2			1	8		
		3		2		7		
		7	3			9		
4	1				7			5
3			5					
9					2			

178

5	2	6		9				
			1		6		3	
		3						
9					8		6	1
	1						8	
7	6		2					3
						7		
	9		6		4			
				7		5	9	8

		7			1		8	
4	1	5	3					
		3		6				1
9			7					
	5						6	
					8			9
7				5		9		
					4	2	1	8
	2		9			4		

		8				9		
			2	7			4	6
						3	2	1
	9			8	6			
		1				4		
			4	2			5	
4	8	3						
7	5			3	9			
		6				2		

	8		6					
	6			4		1	3	
					1	6	7	
8			4					
			9	7	2			
					8			5
	3	1	2					
	7	2		1			5	
					5		4	

			2	8	9			
					6		4	3
7							2	
2		5					9	
	7		5		8		6	
	3					7		1
	1							5
4	9		6					
			3	9	2			

9			3				5	
					7			
	4	1						9
	7			4		8	2	
			5		6			
	5	3		9			4	
1						6	7	
			4					
	3				8			4

6	1		5			8		
		7						9
			8	2				
	6			5				
8	5			6			3	1
				7			6	
			3	9				
3						1		
		9			4		8	2

1
8
5

		5			7		3	
9	4				1	6		
								5
5			9				4	6
		7				9		
1	2				6			8
6								
		1	3				2	9
	8		5			4		

1
8
6

			2					
2				5	9			4
					6	8		7
	1		6	8				2
9								5
3				2	4		7	
1		6	4					
4			3	7				9
				1				

Puzzle 187

9								1
	4		6					
8			3			7	6	
		1	7	3				
	2			1			7	
				8	4	1		
	7	6			2			9
					5		8	
4								5

Puzzle 188

	1	9						
				7			9	8
			6			4	5	
		2				8	4	
1				2				6
	8	4				2		
	6	5			3			
8	7			9				
						1	6	

	6		3				2	
8			2	9				
			6				9	4
1	7							
		3	4		1	8		
							3	7
7	8			6				
			4	9				2
	2			8		6		

					5			
	6	8			4		7	9
			3		7	6		
					9	7		8
	2						5	
4		7	5					
		2	7		6			
5	7		4			8	1	
			2					

7	1	3			8			
9	8				3			7
						5		
		8				3		
			9	2	1			
		4				6		
		2						
4			1				2	6
			8			9	3	5

2		7						
			6				9	3
5				1				7
		6	9			5		8
				3				
9		8			2	7		
8				5				9
4	7				1			
						3		4

Puzzle 193

5	4							
1					6			2
2			8			9		
		5	2	4				
8				3				6
			1	9	5			
		6			4			3
9			3					8
							6	4

Puzzle 194

			1	3	5	2		
			4					1
							9	8
4			6			1		
9		6				5		2
		1			2			3
6	8							
7					4			
		4	7	6	1			

			1		8		7	5
							3	
				2	6	9	1	
	7	3		1				
		8				1		
				7		2	9	
	1	7	9	4				
	6							
3	9		5		2			

						6		8
		8	1					9
		1	7				3	
			9	2			8	6
				4				
9	5			1	7			
	6				3	2		
5					4	3		
3		9						

	8				3			9
	2	3	8					
4		7						2
		5		9				7
			1		2			
2				6		5		
8						7		5
					6	3	1	
5			9				4	

	3				8		6	
		5	3				4	
						7	2	
						4	5	
6	1			3			8	2
	7	2						
	6	8						
	5				1	8		
	9		5				3	

2							3	
				6		2		
		9	8		2		7	5
	2		9			8		
				7				
		5			4		1	
4	6		3		8	9		
		7		5				
	1							6

		6	5		4			2
		2		6		4		7
								3
				7	5			
5			2		6			4
			8	9				
3								
9		8		5		7		
1			6		3	8		

2	4						5	6
				8			7	
7			1	2		3		
					8	9		
				7				
		4	3					
		7		1	6			3
	2			3				
4	6						8	9

				1			2	
1	5				8			9
					2	4		3
		6		8				
		8		7		6		
				5		3		
9		5	8					
8			1				7	2
	3			4				

Puzzle 203

	1			4			8	
			3				2	
		6	2			3		
	2	5			4			7
		7				2		
4			1			8	6	
		3			8	4		
	5				6			
	8			1			9	

Puzzle 204

	3	9						
				1			5	
			7	6	2	8		
	6	3						
1			8	5	9			3
						2	4	
		4	3	8	5			
	7			2				
						4	6	

205

								5
	4		8			1		
	5		7			6		3
			4	5		7		1
				6				
5		4		7	8			
4		7			9		2	
		6			3		8	
9								

206

					1			
			3		4	9		7
		3		8			1	
8		4			2			5
		5				3		
7			1			6		4
	6			7		5		
1		9	4		5			
			9					

					1			
3			6				7	
				7	5	1		8
		3		8			9	5
	8						6	
5	9			1		2		
4		7	9	2				
	2				3			4
			5					

	3		1					
					4	9	1	6
	1							
	8	9			7			2
4			8		5			3
6			3			1	9	
							2	
8	9	7	2					
					6		5	

209

6								
		8	5	4			7	3
		3	1	9				
2			8					6
7					3			5
				8	1	2		
8	7			2	5	1		
								9

210

	7	8	9			1	3	
			1		8			
	5			6				
								5
5	9		4		3		1	2
6								
				9			5	
			3		4			
	8	1			2	7	9	

Puzzle 211

							4	
	5	6				7		
			7		3	2		
3	6	9			5			4
	1						5	
5			1			6	9	8
		2	8		6			
		7				4	1	
	4							

Puzzle 212

6					5			
					7	9		
	3		9	8				5
	8	1				6		
		2	3		6	4		
		5				1	7	
8				2	3		4	
		9	4					
			8					7

213

	6			3				7
			2	6	8	4		
		3			9	8		
						9		
3			7		2			5
		5						
		9	6			3		
		6	3	5	7			
4				9			2	

214

	1			3				
6	7			1	4	9		
		9						
	5	6			9			2
7								5
1			8			4	9	
						7		
		7	2	6			8	4
				4			2	

Puzzle 215

8	9			4	1		7	
2	4							9
							1	
	5				9			
		6	7		5	2		
			8				9	
	8							
5							6	1
	2		6	3			8	7

Puzzle 216

	6	1		5	7			3
		9	8					
		7	2					
	2				4			5
		4				3		
1			9				7	
					5	1		
					9	8		
9			7	3		2	6	

215

216

217

	3			7	1		6	
2								8
		4	5	6		1		
				4			7	
				1				
	7		9					
		5		8	2	6		
1								4
	6		4	3			9	

218

2					5	7		8
7								3
		6	7				1	
			5					2
	3		4		8		9	
6					2			
	8				1	3		
5								6
9		1	3					5

		1				5	6	
			9			8		
	6			3		7		
						3	9	
	1		3	6	7		5	
	2	3						
		9		5			4	
		5			3			
	3	8				6		

3						4		2
			9	2		5		
2	7		5					3
					8		6	
				6				
	3		2					
7					5		8	1
		4		1	9			
8		5						6

						4	8	
	2	1	9					
	6		1				7	
3			4		7			
4			6		2			3
		2			7			9
	9				1		3	
					9	5	6	
	5	8						

2		1						
		7			5	3		
	6		2	4		9		
7			9	2				
		9				6		
				5	7			9
		5		9	3		1	
		3	1			5		
						4		6

		9	5					
					9		3	
6	1					9		2
	6			8		7		1
			2		4			
9		2		1			6	
1		3					5	6
	7		6					
					3	8		

								3
		8	6		9			1
	4	9		5				7
8			1			4		
			2		7			
		2			4			9
1				3		6	7	
2			8		6	3		
4								

Puzzle 225

5		3			7	8		
	4		2	3				1
9								2
		7		8				
			3		1			
				5		4		
1								3
4				6	5		2	
		6	4			1		5

Puzzle 226

		3	1		9			7
		1				3	9	8
					5			
	1	4		2				
	2						3	
				3		6	1	
			9					
5	9	2				4		
8			7		3	1		

227

	8	1		4				
6			3	5			7	
	7	2						
		9						6
		3	5		6	4		
2						8		
						6	9	
	5			2	9			7
				3		1	8	

228

		8	7				2	
	9		3			1		
3			4	6		9		
4		5						
	7						5	
						4		2
		6		7	8			1
		2			4		7	
	5				1	3		

2
2
9

7				3	2	5		1
	4					7		
	8				9			
		9			5			3
	1						2	
5			8			1		
			2				5	
		7					4	
3		4	7	5				8

2
3
0

	1		5			7		
						6	8	9
7	8				2			
			2			1	6	3
4	7	2			1			
			1				7	5
6	4	7						
		5			8		2	

	2	7				9		4
	4							1
1					5	7		
	9			5		8		
				6				
		8		1			4	
		6	8					3
2							1	
7		9				6	8	

2			5	3		6		
			9	4		1		
						9		
5			4				3	1
	1						2	
9	4				7			8
		1						
		7		8	5			
		5		6	3			4

Puzzle 233

	2		4					
		7	2	8				5
		6	9					
	1	8				2		
	6	3				9	4	
		4				6	5	
					1	3		
8				7	6	1		
					9		7	

Puzzle 234

1				7	4		6	
4							3	
8					3			
		9		2			5	
3			6		5			4
	6			4		2		
			1					5
	8							9
	3		7	6				2

5					1			
8		1	5				4	
	3	9					6	
	6	4		9			8	
	5			4		2	1	
	2					4	9	
	9				3	1		5
			8					7

8	7							
		5						4
	1		7			5	9	
	6		2			8		3
			6		8			
3		8			9		2	
	8	6			5		4	
2						1		
							7	9

	4				3	5		
2		3				4		6
					9		1	
			2					7
			7	8	6			
5					4			
	3		9					
6		5				7		4
		9	1				8	

		5			8			
7				3	6	4	1	
	9						2	
9			6	8		2		
		2		1	4			7
	3						7	
	6	4	5	9				8
			8			6		

Puzzle 239

	7				4	3	2	6
4				8				
		9			7			
			8			9		
		4	1		2	5		
		2			3			
			4			7		
				5				9
6	4	1	2				5	

Puzzle 240

						5		6
				4	2	9		8
			8					4
				1		4	6	
5		6				7		3
	9	1		7				
7					1			
1		2	6	3				
6		8						

	8			3		1	6	
		2					4	
		5	1					8
				7				9
		7		5		2		
4				1				
6					8	7		
	5					6		
	3	9		2			1	

	5		1				7	
			3					9
3		1	7					8
	8	7						2
6								1
4						7	9	
9					6	4		3
2					4			
	4				7		1	

7	5			2				
	2					4		9
		3		8	6			2
6								
			5	9	2			
								8
5			4	3		7		
1		8					9	
				5			3	1

			5					6
1		3				2		
2		7		6				3
9		4			7			
	1						9	
			8			5		1
7				8		3		2
		2				7		5
5					4			

2 4 5

							9	
2							4	6
		7	4		5	2		
3		5	2					7
			8		7			
7					3	1		4
		8	9		1	5		
6	2							3
	1							

2 4 6

	5	3						
							2	
4				5		8		7
8			2				6	9
6				1				5
3	4				6			2
7		9		4				6
	1							
						1	4	

	4	8						
			2		9			1
		6				3	7	9
			8					5
6	1						9	2
7					6			
5	7	3				6		
4			1		7			
						2	3	

	7					6		
		2			1			
			3	9	5		8	
1	9				7		2	
2								3
	6		8				5	4
	5		4	8	6			
			1			9		
		6					7	

Puzzle 249

	9		7			3	1	
7			2			8		
6								
		3		6				
8	2						3	5
				7		2		
								4
		4			9			6
	6	1			4		7	

Puzzle 250

	9		8				4	
			1				2	9
6		1	5					
3	1							
	5		2		1		7	
							1	4
					5	8		6
8	3				9			
	2				7		9	

3		5	8					1
			4				6	
				9		4	2	
	5		2		7		4	
	6		5		8		7	
	3	6		5				
	7				1			
5					6	9		3

8	9						5	
	4			6				
3			7		2			
2					1			3
1	3						2	7
5			3					8
			6		4			1
				7			6	
	1						9	5

					1		3	2
				3			4	
			5	8			6	
6			8			1	9	
				7				
	1	9			3			5
	8			4	5			
	7			1				
1	2		9					

8	2		9			7	1	
				7				
	6		8		5			2
	4	5			8			
			1			2	5	
6			5		1		9	
				6				
	8	1			9		2	3

255

9				1	8		2	
	3	7						
		6			5			
	1					5		3
	6						4	
8		2					6	
			5			1		
						7	9	
	5		6	8				4

256

	2							1
		4	6	3			5	2
				1	2	8		3
					4			
	1						3	
			7					
8		2	4	5				
3	9			7	8	6		
7							9	

7				3				
	5				1		2	
		4	6			1		7
5	8							
	2			5			6	
							5	4
2		6			8	7		
	9		2				8	
				9				2

		8				3		
6		9		8				5
4					6		8	
				4	8		9	3
7	5		2	3				
	2		7					8
1				2		9		4
		6				5		

		6						7
9					3	1		2
1							3	
4	2			1				
		5	8		4	9		
				3			1	5
	3							9
7		8	2					6
2						5		

		6				1	7	
			5				3	
7						9		6
9		1		4				
5			3		2			9
				8		2		4
2		4						1
	6				8			
	3	5				4		

			7				9	
6	3	4		8				
		1						2
5	7					1		
	8			6			3	
		9					7	5
4						2		
				1		4	5	3
	2				3			

		5	3					
		4		7				
6		9		8	1			
1	5						7	
		6	1		2	9		
	9						3	8
			2	1		8		5
				9		6		
					6	3		

263

				8	1	7		
			2		6			5
	8							9
		2		7		6		
6	9						3	1
		4		1		8		
4							5	
9			4		2			
		1	9	3				

264

		6	3					
				1	9		7	
3							2	
5					1		9	7
		8	4		2	5		
1	9		6					2
	4							1
	5		2	4				
					8	4		

7		9						
		4			9	7		
2			8				1	9
						6		3
	3			2			5	
1		8						
8	9				7			2
		7	3			4		
						1		6

			2					6
1	3		5				4	
		2				5	3	
					4		1	3
			3		7			
5	9		1					
	4	1				9		
	5				2		7	8
3					6			

	2				5		7	
			8	1	4			
	6					1		
	4			8	3		5	
		7				9		
	5		1	4			6	
		5					1	
			3	9	2			
	9		6				4	

						5		
8			7					3
3			1	5		4		
	1			9	5		4	
6								2
	4		2	3			7	
		9		1	3			5
7					8			4
		5						

	1		4					7
		5	9				3	1
			2		6			
		2	8					5
		9			3			
1			5		4			
		1	3					
9	7				2	5		
5					1		8	

			4				8	1
		4		1				5
3	6		9					
	9		3				7	8
6	5				4		9	
					1		6	3
1				8		4		
8	4				7			

	5	1			9	7	6	
	8		6					
							9	
4					7	1	5	
		8				2		
	6	7	8					9
	9							
					6		4	
	2	4	9			5	8	

			1				9	
7			9		8			
6	2							
		7		1		4		5
		2	3		4	7		
4		3		6		1		
							4	2
			4		7			3
	5				9			

			9	8		2		
8	6					5		4
		3		4				
					7	1		6
9								5
7		6	8					
				5		4		
6		9					1	2
		4		1	3			

				2		1	9	
			6		9			
4				8			7	3
2		8	9			7		
		5			2	8		4
5	7			6				8
			7		4			
	2	1		3				

	6					4	8	1
1				2		9		
	7	8					6	
			2					
		3	9		5	2		
					6			
	1					7	2	
		7		4				6
3	8	2					1	

			6		2	9		3
			3	4		5		6
	7							
					4	2		
8	9						3	1
		1	5					
							9	
5		6		9	3			
9		8	2		1			

6		7		5	8			1
					9	3	5	
		1						
	9			7		8		
			9		2			
		8		1			6	
						4		
	7	9	5					
8			3	2		5		6

1					3			8
	2		8	9				
6	8			5		3	9	
								9
	7						6	
8								
	9	1		7			8	2
				2	9		1	
3			4					6

Puzzle 279

			2			4		
7						5		6
			6		1		9	
	8						2	1
			3	2	8			
4	9						5	
	7		4		2			
1		3						9
		6			7			

Puzzle 280

	7	5		2	9	1		
9			3			2		5
8								
						6		9
3		1						
								3
5		6			4			7
		3	2	1		8	5	

144

	4	1		6			5	
				7	3	8		
	5		8					
	3			1				6
		6				7		
2				5			3	
					6		8	
		3	9	8				
	8			3		4	2	

5	7					8	6	
						7		5
	3		5		2			
7						4	9	
				3				
	9	4						1
			4		6		2	
4		8						
	1	9					7	4

8			6	3		1		
	3				2		8	5
		6	1					
						7	2	
			4		9			
	4	1						
					5	8		
3	9		2				6	
		5		9	7			3

					6	5		
8	4						6	
		9	1		8			4
	6			2				
		1		9		2		
				5			3	
2			5		9	3		
	1						5	6
		3	7					

		4						
	1	2	9			8	7	
7	5							3
		1			4		8	
		3				7		
	9		2			1		
6							4	5
	8	9			3	6	1	
						2		

7			5	8		2	6	
		3						
5		6	1				4	
4				9				
		5				1		
				7				9
	2				4	8		7
						4		
	7	4		3	2			1

287

			7		6			
					1		6	3
7		6						8
					7		5	
	9	1				2	3	
	2		4					
8						9		2
2	4		3					
			1		4			

288

	4	8		5				1
		9						
			8	7		3		4
		3				8	9	
				1				
	2	6				5		
8		2		6	7			
						1		
5				4		7	2	

289

	2	8				3		
	7	9	4					
3	1			7				
						5	7	
	3		6		4		9	
	5	6						
				1			3	9
					9	2	5	
		2				1	6	

290

			3			8	6	7
		8		6			4	
		7	9					5
			8					
	4	5				3	1	
					9			
8					1	5		
	3			7		6		
6	2	4			3			

2				8				3
6		7	1				4	9
	4	5		3	2			
		2				7		
			4	9		5	2	
8	6				3	1		7
1				4				6

				6		3		
	1			9	7			2
6		4	8					
		7	5			9		
		3				5		
		6			1	7		
					9	6		3
4			6	1			8	
		1		2				

5			1			8		4
		4	3		6		1	
			8	7				
		5					6	
	4						3	
	1					9		
				2	7			
	3		9		5	1		
9		6			1			7

1							2	4
	6		5			1	7	
		3	2					
3	5							
		2				5		
							4	9
					3	6		
		4	9		6		5	
7	2							3

7		5						2
			2			9		
2					8	1		
		6			1		3	8
				3				
5	4		9			6		
		1	4					3
		4			2			
3						5		9

				6				2
	3		8			7	9	
			4			6		5
			2					
	9			7			5	
					5			
4		5			2			
	7	1			8		3	
6				9				

Puzzle 297

	8					7		1
4	6		9			8		
		5						
3		9	6					
				5				
					7	2		3
						9		
		8			2		1	5
6		7					3	

Puzzle 298

1					2			
			4			6		
		5	9		3			
	4						3	
7	6			3			9	4
	8						5	
			8		4	1		
		2			5			
			6					3

		9		2	3			
	7	6					4	3
								1
					6			7
			1	8	4			
8			7					
1								
5	6					9	8	
			8	3		4		

						1		
			8		9			
			6	5			3	4
				3		4	5	
		1				8		
	6	8		7				
3	8			2	7			
			5		4			
		7						

1

1	5	9	2	7	6	3	8	4
4	8	7	3	9	5	1	6	2
2	6	3	8	1	4	9	5	7
7	2	4	5	8	9	6	1	3
8	9	1	7	6	3	2	4	5
5	3	6	1	4	2	8	7	9
6	1	2	4	3	7	5	9	8
3	4	8	9	5	1	7	2	6
9	7	5	6	2	8	4	3	1

2

6	4	7	8	5	2	1	3	9
5	8	1	6	3	9	4	7	2
2	3	9	1	4	7	5	6	8
8	1	6	5	9	4	3	2	7
4	2	3	7	8	1	6	9	5
9	7	5	3	2	6	8	1	4
1	9	8	4	7	3	2	5	6
3	5	2	9	6	8	7	4	1
7	6	4	2	1	5	9	8	3

3

4	5	9	6	7	3	2	8	1
2	8	7	9	4	1	6	3	5
1	3	6	2	5	8	7	4	9
9	2	3	5	6	7	8	1	4
7	1	5	8	3	4	9	2	6
8	6	4	1	2	9	5	7	3
6	7	2	4	1	5	3	9	8
3	4	8	7	9	6	1	5	2
5	9	1	3	8	2	4	6	7

4

1	7	9	5	6	2	8	4	3
5	3	4	7	8	9	2	6	1
2	8	6	3	1	4	5	9	7
9	2	3	4	7	8	6	1	5
8	6	5	9	3	1	7	2	4
7	4	1	2	5	6	3	8	9
3	1	8	6	9	5	4	7	2
4	9	7	8	2	3	1	5	6
6	5	2	1	4	7	9	3	8

5

9	8	2	7	1	5	6	4	3
7	3	6	2	8	4	5	1	9
5	1	4	3	6	9	7	8	2
1	9	7	4	5	2	3	6	8
3	2	5	6	9	8	4	7	1
4	6	8	1	7	3	9	2	5
8	7	3	5	2	6	1	9	4
2	5	1	9	4	7	8	3	6
6	4	9	8	3	1	2	5	7

6

9	5	6	4	8	3	7	2	1
4	7	1	2	9	5	8	3	6
8	2	3	1	6	7	5	9	4
1	3	5	6	2	9	4	7	8
7	9	8	3	4	1	2	6	5
6	4	2	7	5	8	3	1	9
3	8	9	5	1	2	6	4	7
2	1	4	8	7	6	9	5	3
5	6	7	9	3	4	1	8	2

7

9	4	8	6	2	3	7	1	5
1	2	5	7	4	9	6	3	8
6	7	3	8	1	5	2	9	4
4	5	9	2	3	6	1	8	7
7	8	2	9	5	1	4	6	3
3	6	1	4	7	8	5	2	9
2	9	6	5	8	4	3	7	1
8	1	4	3	6	7	9	5	2
5	3	7	1	9	2	8	4	6

8

8	4	3	7	2	5	1	9	6
9	1	5	4	8	6	7	3	2
7	2	6	3	9	1	8	4	5
4	7	8	1	5	2	3	6	9
6	3	9	8	7	4	5	2	1
2	5	1	6	3	9	4	7	8
5	8	4	2	6	7	9	1	3
3	6	7	9	1	8	2	5	4
1	9	2	5	4	3	6	8	7

9

5	6	1	3	4	8	7	2	9
2	7	9	6	1	5	3	8	4
8	4	3	9	7	2	5	6	1
7	2	8	1	9	4	6	5	3
9	1	6	7	5	3	2	4	8
4	3	5	8	2	6	1	9	7
3	8	4	5	6	1	9	7	2
6	9	2	4	3	7	8	1	5
1	5	7	2	8	9	4	3	6

10

9	5	8	2	6	4	1	3	7
6	7	1	8	3	9	5	2	4
4	2	3	7	1	5	8	9	6
2	4	6	5	9	1	7	8	3
3	8	5	6	7	2	4	1	9
1	9	7	4	8	3	6	5	2
5	1	2	9	4	7	3	6	8
7	6	9	3	5	8	2	4	1
8	3	4	1	2	6	9	7	5

11

1	9	8	3	5	4	7	2	6
2	6	5	7	8	9	1	3	4
4	3	7	1	2	6	9	5	8
6	2	4	9	3	5	8	1	7
7	8	3	6	4	1	5	9	2
5	1	9	2	7	8	4	6	3
3	4	1	8	9	2	6	7	5
8	7	6	5	1	3	2	4	9
9	5	2	4	6	7	3	8	1

12

2	4	3	7	1	6	5	8	9
5	6	9	3	4	8	2	7	1
8	1	7	2	5	9	4	3	6
1	7	6	5	2	4	8	9	3
3	2	5	8	9	1	6	4	7
9	8	4	6	3	7	1	5	2
7	3	8	1	6	5	9	2	4
4	5	1	9	7	2	3	6	8
6	9	2	4	8	3	7	1	5

13

4	1	8	5	7	2	9	6	3
2	7	9	1	6	3	5	4	8
5	6	3	9	8	4	7	2	1
3	4	1	7	2	6	8	9	5
8	2	7	4	5	9	1	3	6
6	9	5	8	3	1	4	7	2
1	8	2	6	4	7	3	5	9
7	5	6	3	9	8	2	1	4
9	3	4	2	1	5	6	8	7

14

4	5	6	8	2	9	7	3	1
1	7	9	5	4	3	8	2	6
3	8	2	1	7	6	5	9	4
5	6	8	7	3	4	9	1	2
9	3	1	2	6	5	4	7	8
7	2	4	9	8	1	3	6	5
6	4	7	3	1	8	2	5	9
2	1	5	4	9	7	6	8	3
8	9	3	6	5	2	1	4	7

15

1	7	3	5	6	4	9	2	8
4	8	2	9	1	3	7	5	6
6	9	5	7	8	2	4	1	3
2	1	9	8	3	6	5	7	4
3	5	8	4	7	1	2	6	9
7	4	6	2	9	5	8	3	1
8	3	7	1	2	9	6	4	5
5	2	1	6	4	8	3	9	7
9	6	4	3	5	7	1	8	2

16

9	4	5	8	2	7	3	1	6
6	3	8	1	9	5	7	2	4
2	1	7	4	6	3	5	9	8
4	5	3	7	8	1	9	6	2
7	6	2	3	4	9	1	8	5
8	9	1	6	5	2	4	3	7
5	8	9	2	1	4	6	7	3
1	7	6	5	3	8	2	4	9
3	2	4	9	7	6	8	5	1

17

8	4	6	1	3	5	9	7	2
9	2	7	6	8	4	5	3	1
1	3	5	2	9	7	4	8	6
6	8	4	5	7	9	1	2	3
3	9	1	4	6	2	7	5	8
5	7	2	3	1	8	6	9	4
2	5	3	9	4	6	8	1	7
4	1	8	7	5	3	2	6	9
7	6	9	8	2	1	3	4	5

18

3	8	9	2	1	4	5	6	7
6	5	2	7	3	9	8	4	1
7	4	1	6	8	5	9	2	3
8	6	3	9	4	2	1	7	5
2	9	4	5	7	1	6	3	8
5	1	7	3	6	8	4	9	2
4	2	6	8	5	7	3	1	9
9	3	8	1	2	6	7	5	4
1	7	5	4	9	3	2	8	6

19

5	6	4	3	2	8	9	7	1
3	8	1	7	5	9	6	2	4
7	9	2	6	4	1	5	8	3
6	7	8	2	9	4	3	1	5
1	2	3	5	6	7	8	4	9
9	4	5	8	1	3	2	6	7
4	5	6	9	7	2	1	3	8
2	3	7	1	8	5	4	9	6
8	1	9	4	3	6	7	5	2

20

2	5	6	4	9	1	3	7	8
8	1	4	5	7	3	6	9	2
9	7	3	6	8	2	5	1	4
6	3	5	7	2	9	4	8	1
4	8	2	3	1	5	9	6	7
7	9	1	8	6	4	2	3	5
3	6	8	2	4	7	1	5	9
5	2	9	1	3	8	7	4	6
1	4	7	9	5	6	8	2	3

21

3	7	6	9	2	5	1	8	4
2	5	1	4	3	8	9	6	7
8	9	4	1	6	7	3	2	5
1	3	2	8	7	4	6	5	9
7	8	9	3	5	6	2	4	1
4	6	5	2	9	1	8	7	3
5	2	7	6	1	3	4	9	8
9	4	3	7	8	2	5	1	6
6	1	8	5	4	9	7	3	2

22

8	1	3	9	6	5	2	7	4
6	5	9	4	2	7	1	3	8
7	4	2	8	3	1	5	6	9
9	7	5	3	4	2	8	1	6
4	2	6	5	1	8	7	9	3
3	8	1	7	9	6	4	2	5
5	6	8	1	7	9	3	4	2
2	3	7	6	5	4	9	8	1
1	9	4	2	8	3	6	5	7

23

6	9	8	3	7	2	5	1	4
5	4	7	9	8	1	3	2	6
3	1	2	6	4	5	7	8	9
7	2	4	1	9	6	8	3	5
1	6	3	2	5	8	4	9	7
8	5	9	4	3	7	2	6	1
4	8	6	7	2	9	1	5	3
9	7	5	8	1	3	6	4	2
2	3	1	5	6	4	9	7	8

24

6	8	3	2	5	9	4	1	7
4	7	9	8	3	1	5	6	2
2	1	5	7	4	6	8	9	3
1	6	7	5	2	3	9	4	8
3	9	8	4	1	7	2	5	6
5	4	2	9	6	8	3	7	1
8	5	6	3	7	4	1	2	9
7	3	4	1	9	2	6	8	5
9	2	1	6	8	5	7	3	4

25

1	2	4	5	8	3	7	6	9
3	7	6	2	9	4	5	8	1
9	8	5	7	1	6	2	3	4
8	5	3	4	7	2	9	1	6
4	9	2	6	3	1	8	7	5
7	6	1	9	5	8	3	4	2
2	1	8	3	6	5	4	9	7
5	3	7	1	4	9	6	2	8
6	4	9	8	2	7	1	5	3

26

8	1	3	5	9	2	7	4	6
9	5	4	1	7	6	3	8	2
7	6	2	8	4	3	1	5	9
6	9	7	4	1	8	5	2	3
4	3	5	7	2	9	6	1	8
2	8	1	3	6	5	9	7	4
5	4	6	2	3	7	8	9	1
3	2	8	9	5	1	4	6	7
1	7	9	6	8	4	2	3	5

27

9	2	6	1	5	3	7	8	4
3	8	1	7	9	4	6	2	5
4	7	5	8	2	6	1	3	9
6	3	2	9	7	1	4	5	8
5	4	8	6	3	2	9	7	1
1	9	7	5	4	8	3	6	2
8	1	4	2	6	7	5	9	3
2	6	9	3	1	5	8	4	7
7	5	3	4	8	9	2	1	6

28

5	6	4	7	8	9	1	3	2
7	3	9	1	2	6	4	8	5
2	8	1	4	5	3	9	7	6
9	7	6	2	3	1	5	4	8
8	1	3	6	4	5	2	9	7
4	5	2	8	9	7	3	6	1
1	2	8	9	6	4	7	5	3
6	4	5	3	7	2	8	1	9
3	9	7	5	1	8	6	2	4

29

1	8	5	2	7	4	6	3	9
7	3	2	9	6	1	5	8	4
6	4	9	3	8	5	7	2	1
9	6	1	5	2	8	4	7	3
2	5	8	7	4	3	9	1	6
3	7	4	6	1	9	2	5	8
4	1	7	8	5	6	3	9	2
8	2	3	4	9	7	1	6	5
5	9	6	1	3	2	8	4	7

30

4	7	1	2	6	3	9	8	5
9	6	8	7	4	5	1	3	2
3	2	5	8	9	1	7	6	4
6	8	2	4	3	7	5	1	9
1	9	3	5	8	2	6	4	7
5	4	7	9	1	6	3	2	8
8	5	6	3	7	4	2	9	1
7	1	9	6	2	8	4	5	3
2	3	4	1	5	9	8	7	6

31

1	6	8	3	5	2	4	7	9
9	7	4	1	8	6	3	5	2
5	3	2	4	7	9	1	8	6
6	9	5	8	1	7	2	3	4
8	2	7	9	4	3	5	6	1
3	4	1	6	2	5	8	9	7
4	8	9	5	6	1	7	2	3
7	5	3	2	9	4	6	1	8
2	1	6	7	3	8	9	4	5

32

7	9	1	4	6	3	8	2	5
3	8	4	2	7	5	9	1	6
5	2	6	9	1	8	3	4	7
2	5	7	3	4	6	1	9	8
9	4	3	8	5	1	6	7	2
6	1	8	7	9	2	4	5	3
8	3	9	5	2	4	7	6	1
1	7	5	6	3	9	2	8	4
4	6	2	1	8	7	5	3	9

3 3

9	2	3	6	7	1	4	8	5
1	7	4	5	8	2	9	3	6
6	5	8	3	4	9	1	7	2
3	4	6	2	5	7	8	1	9
5	1	7	8	9	4	2	6	3
8	9	2	1	6	3	7	5	4
7	8	5	9	2	6	3	4	1
4	3	9	7	1	5	6	2	8
2	6	1	4	3	8	5	9	7

3 4

5	9	2	8	4	6	3	1	7
6	4	7	1	5	3	9	2	8
3	8	1	7	9	2	5	4	6
2	7	6	9	8	5	4	3	1
9	3	8	2	1	4	6	7	5
4	1	5	6	3	7	8	9	2
8	5	9	3	7	1	2	6	4
1	6	3	4	2	8	7	5	9
7	2	4	5	6	9	1	8	3

3 5

5	6	7	3	8	2	4	9	1
2	9	8	6	1	4	5	7	3
1	3	4	9	7	5	8	6	2
4	7	1	5	9	3	2	8	6
8	2	3	1	6	7	9	5	4
9	5	6	2	4	8	1	3	7
6	4	9	7	5	1	3	2	8
3	8	5	4	2	6	7	1	9
7	1	2	8	3	9	6	4	5

3 6

3	6	9	2	1	8	5	4	7
1	8	2	5	7	4	3	9	6
4	5	7	6	3	9	8	1	2
2	3	4	7	9	5	6	8	1
6	1	8	3	4	2	9	7	5
9	7	5	8	6	1	4	2	3
8	2	3	4	5	7	1	6	9
7	9	6	1	8	3	2	5	4
5	4	1	9	2	6	7	3	8

3 7

6	7	9	5	3	2	8	4	1
5	3	2	4	1	8	7	9	6
1	8	4	7	6	9	2	3	5
2	4	3	6	5	1	9	7	8
7	6	1	8	9	4	5	2	3
9	5	8	2	7	3	6	1	4
8	9	7	3	4	5	1	6	2
4	1	5	9	2	6	3	8	7
3	2	6	1	8	7	4	5	9

3 8

4	2	7	1	8	6	5	3	9
1	6	8	9	5	3	4	2	7
9	5	3	4	2	7	1	6	8
7	9	2	5	1	4	6	8	3
6	1	5	8	3	9	7	4	2
8	3	4	6	7	2	9	5	1
2	7	6	3	4	1	8	9	5
5	4	1	2	9	8	3	7	6
3	8	9	7	6	5	2	1	4

3 9

1	2	3	4	9	6	7	5	8
5	6	7	1	3	8	9	4	2
4	9	8	2	7	5	1	6	3
8	5	9	7	2	3	4	1	6
6	7	1	5	8	4	3	2	9
2	3	4	9	6	1	5	8	7
3	4	2	6	5	9	8	7	1
9	1	6	8	4	7	2	3	5
7	8	5	3	1	2	6	9	4

4 0

1	8	9	7	2	4	5	6	3
4	5	3	1	8	6	9	7	2
7	2	6	5	9	3	1	4	8
9	1	4	6	3	7	2	8	5
2	6	7	8	5	9	4	3	1
5	3	8	2	4	1	7	9	6
6	7	5	4	1	8	3	2	9
3	4	1	9	6	2	8	5	7
8	9	2	3	7	5	6	1	4

4-1

8	2	1	9	7	3	4	5	6
5	6	9	2	4	1	7	3	8
4	3	7	8	6	5	9	2	1
3	5	6	7	8	9	2	1	4
1	7	4	3	5	2	8	6	9
9	8	2	4	1	6	5	7	3
2	9	5	1	3	8	6	4	7
7	1	8	6	2	4	3	9	5
6	4	3	5	9	7	1	8	2

4-2

3	5	6	7	8	9	4	2	1
4	8	9	1	2	6	5	3	7
7	2	1	3	4	5	6	9	8
8	6	7	9	5	3	2	1	4
1	4	3	8	6	2	7	5	9
5	9	2	4	1	7	8	6	3
9	7	5	6	3	8	1	4	2
6	3	4	2	7	1	9	8	5
2	1	8	5	9	4	3	7	6

4-3

6	5	1	3	2	4	9	8	7
9	3	8	6	7	5	2	4	1
7	2	4	8	1	9	5	6	3
1	8	2	9	3	7	4	5	6
4	7	5	1	8	6	3	2	9
3	9	6	5	4	2	7	1	8
5	6	3	4	9	8	1	7	2
8	1	7	2	5	3	6	9	4
2	4	9	7	6	1	8	3	5

4-4

3	4	1	7	9	6	5	2	8
2	9	8	5	4	3	6	7	1
5	7	6	8	2	1	9	4	3
8	3	5	9	1	4	2	6	7
9	6	7	3	8	2	1	5	4
1	2	4	6	5	7	8	3	9
4	8	2	1	7	5	3	9	6
7	1	3	2	6	9	4	8	5
6	5	9	4	3	8	7	1	2

4-5

3	6	9	4	5	2	1	7	8
1	5	4	9	7	8	6	3	2
2	8	7	1	3	6	9	4	5
6	4	3	2	9	5	8	1	7
7	2	5	8	1	4	3	6	9
9	1	8	3	6	7	2	5	4
4	9	1	5	8	3	7	2	6
8	7	2	6	4	1	5	9	3
5	3	6	7	2	9	4	8	1

4-6

6	1	9	4	5	7	8	3	2
4	8	7	9	2	3	5	6	1
5	2	3	6	1	8	4	7	9
1	4	2	5	8	6	7	9	3
3	5	6	7	9	1	2	4	8
9	7	8	2	3	4	1	5	6
2	9	1	3	7	5	6	8	4
7	3	4	8	6	2	9	1	5
8	6	5	1	4	9	3	2	7

4-7

6	9	3	2	8	7	5	4	1
1	8	7	4	5	3	2	9	6
4	5	2	6	9	1	3	8	7
8	2	5	7	3	9	1	6	4
7	1	4	5	2	6	9	3	8
9	3	6	1	4	8	7	5	2
5	6	9	8	1	2	4	7	3
2	4	8	3	7	5	6	1	9
3	7	1	9	6	4	8	2	5

4-8

1	6	4	2	9	5	3	8	7
8	2	9	4	7	3	5	6	1
5	3	7	1	8	6	2	4	9
3	9	1	8	6	2	7	5	4
6	7	2	9	5	4	1	3	8
4	8	5	7	3	1	9	2	6
2	4	8	3	1	9	6	7	5
7	1	6	5	2	8	4	9	3
9	5	3	6	4	7	8	1	2

49

3	7	2	6	8	5	1	9	4
9	4	6	7	1	3	5	2	8
5	8	1	9	4	2	3	7	6
6	1	3	2	9	7	8	4	5
2	9	8	1	5	4	6	3	7
7	5	4	3	6	8	2	1	9
4	2	9	5	3	6	7	8	1
8	6	7	4	2	1	9	5	3
1	3	5	8	7	9	4	6	2

50

7	2	1	5	4	6	8	3	9
5	6	8	9	1	3	2	7	4
3	9	4	8	7	2	6	1	5
2	1	3	4	6	7	5	9	8
9	4	5	1	3	8	7	2	6
8	7	6	2	9	5	3	4	1
4	3	7	6	8	1	9	5	2
6	5	9	3	2	4	1	8	7
1	8	2	7	5	9	4	6	3

51

7	9	4	6	1	2	3	5	8
8	1	6	7	5	3	4	9	2
3	2	5	9	8	4	1	6	7
6	7	8	5	4	1	9	2	3
5	4	1	2	3	9	8	7	6
9	3	2	8	6	7	5	4	1
2	6	3	1	9	5	7	8	4
4	5	7	3	2	8	6	1	9
1	8	9	4	7	6	2	3	5

52

2	5	6	7	8	3	9	4	1
7	8	4	1	5	9	3	2	6
3	1	9	6	2	4	7	8	5
5	3	7	8	4	1	2	6	9
4	9	8	5	6	2	1	3	7
6	2	1	9	3	7	8	5	4
9	6	2	3	1	5	4	7	8
8	7	3	4	9	6	5	1	2
1	4	5	2	7	8	6	9	3

53

2	8	1	6	5	4	7	9	3
4	3	9	8	7	2	5	6	1
7	6	5	1	3	9	4	2	8
9	7	3	5	2	8	1	4	6
1	4	6	3	9	7	2	8	5
5	2	8	4	6	1	9	3	7
3	9	7	2	1	6	8	5	4
8	5	2	7	4	3	6	1	9
6	1	4	9	8	5	3	7	2

54

6	1	9	8	2	4	5	3	7
5	3	7	1	6	9	2	8	4
8	2	4	7	5	3	9	6	1
3	4	1	2	7	5	8	9	6
2	5	6	9	1	8	7	4	3
9	7	8	3	4	6	1	2	5
7	6	5	4	8	2	3	1	9
1	9	2	6	3	7	4	5	8
4	8	3	5	9	1	6	7	2

55

6	2	7	9	3	8	1	5	4
5	9	3	6	1	4	2	8	7
4	8	1	2	7	5	3	6	9
9	5	2	4	6	1	8	7	3
8	7	4	3	9	2	6	1	5
3	1	6	5	8	7	4	9	2
2	6	8	7	4	9	5	3	1
7	3	5	1	2	6	9	4	8
1	4	9	8	5	3	7	2	6

56

4	7	2	6	3	9	8	5	1
9	6	1	8	4	5	7	3	2
8	5	3	1	2	7	6	9	4
5	3	4	9	7	8	2	1	6
2	9	6	3	1	4	5	7	8
1	8	7	2	5	6	9	4	3
6	1	5	4	9	2	3	8	7
3	2	9	7	8	1	4	6	5
7	4	8	5	6	3	1	2	9

57

1	6	8	4	3	9	7	2	5
4	5	9	2	7	1	6	8	3
7	3	2	5	6	8	4	9	1
6	9	1	3	8	4	2	5	7
5	8	7	6	1	2	9	3	4
2	4	3	9	5	7	8	1	6
9	2	6	1	4	5	3	7	8
3	7	5	8	2	6	1	4	9
8	1	4	7	9	3	5	6	2

58

7	4	8	9	2	5	1	3	6
2	9	3	1	6	4	7	8	5
6	1	5	7	3	8	9	2	4
3	6	9	8	7	1	4	5	2
1	2	4	3	5	9	6	7	8
8	5	7	6	4	2	3	1	9
4	7	6	2	8	3	5	9	1
5	8	1	4	9	7	2	6	3
9	3	2	5	1	6	8	4	7

59

2	1	3	6	4	8	9	5	7
8	7	5	2	9	1	4	6	3
6	9	4	3	5	7	8	2	1
3	2	6	4	7	9	1	8	5
7	5	1	8	2	3	6	4	9
9	4	8	1	6	5	7	3	2
4	3	9	5	1	6	2	7	8
5	6	7	9	8	2	3	1	4
1	8	2	7	3	4	5	9	6

60

1	2	8	7	9	4	6	3	5
9	3	7	6	5	8	2	1	4
4	6	5	2	3	1	7	8	9
6	8	4	9	2	3	1	5	7
2	5	1	4	8	7	3	9	6
3	7	9	1	6	5	8	4	2
5	4	2	8	1	6	9	7	3
8	9	3	5	7	2	4	6	1
7	1	6	3	4	9	5	2	8

61

1	4	7	8	5	6	9	3	2
6	5	2	4	3	9	7	1	8
8	9	3	1	2	7	4	5	6
7	8	9	5	6	3	1	2	4
2	6	1	9	8	4	5	7	3
5	3	4	7	1	2	6	8	9
9	7	8	3	4	5	2	6	1
3	2	5	6	9	1	8	4	7
4	1	6	2	7	8	3	9	5

62

9	2	3	5	8	7	6	4	1
6	8	1	2	4	3	7	5	9
4	7	5	6	9	1	8	3	2
7	6	4	9	3	2	5	1	8
3	1	9	7	5	8	4	2	6
8	5	2	1	6	4	9	7	3
5	3	7	8	1	9	2	6	4
1	9	6	4	2	5	3	8	7
2	4	8	3	7	6	1	9	5

63

1	6	5	8	7	2	3	9	4
2	9	4	1	3	5	7	8	6
3	8	7	6	9	4	2	1	5
4	2	1	5	6	7	8	3	9
9	7	6	4	8	3	1	5	2
8	5	3	9	2	1	4	6	7
6	1	2	3	4	9	5	7	8
5	4	9	7	1	8	6	2	3
7	3	8	2	5	6	9	4	1

64

4	9	2	1	3	7	8	5	6
5	3	1	6	2	8	7	4	9
6	8	7	5	9	4	2	1	3
7	6	8	9	5	2	1	3	4
2	5	3	4	7	1	9	6	8
9	1	4	3	8	6	5	7	2
1	7	9	8	4	3	6	2	5
8	4	6	2	1	5	3	9	7
3	2	5	7	6	9	4	8	1

6/5

1	8	6	5	9	2	3	7	4
4	7	2	1	3	8	9	5	6
9	5	3	4	7	6	2	8	1
5	1	7	2	4	3	8	6	9
6	3	4	7	8	9	5	1	2
2	9	8	6	1	5	7	4	3
7	2	9	8	6	1	4	3	5
3	4	1	9	5	7	6	2	8
8	6	5	3	2	4	1	9	7

6/6

2	4	6	9	1	5	8	3	7
5	1	8	4	7	3	6	9	2
9	7	3	8	6	2	4	5	1
6	8	5	2	9	7	1	4	3
7	3	4	1	5	8	9	2	6
1	9	2	3	4	6	7	8	5
3	6	1	5	8	9	2	7	4
4	5	9	7	2	1	3	6	8
8	2	7	6	3	4	5	1	9

6/7

8	5	3	2	6	7	1	9	4
7	6	9	1	8	4	3	2	5
4	2	1	9	5	3	8	7	6
3	4	8	6	7	9	2	5	1
5	1	6	3	2	8	9	4	7
2	9	7	4	1	5	6	8	3
6	7	2	5	9	1	4	3	8
1	3	5	8	4	2	7	6	9
9	8	4	7	3	6	5	1	2

6/8

4	6	3	2	8	5	1	9	7
2	1	9	6	7	3	8	5	4
7	5	8	1	9	4	6	3	2
1	9	7	3	4	6	5	2	8
8	4	6	9	5	2	7	1	3
3	2	5	7	1	8	9	4	6
6	8	1	4	2	9	3	7	5
9	3	2	5	6	7	4	8	1
5	7	4	8	3	1	2	6	9

6/9

1	2	9	8	6	3	5	4	7
6	8	4	7	9	5	1	2	3
5	7	3	1	2	4	8	9	6
3	1	6	9	4	8	7	5	2
8	4	7	6	5	2	9	3	1
2	9	5	3	7	1	6	8	4
4	3	8	5	1	6	2	7	9
9	6	2	4	8	7	3	1	5
7	5	1	2	3	9	4	6	8

7/0

8	6	5	9	3	7	1	2	4
9	1	4	5	2	6	3	7	8
7	2	3	4	1	8	6	5	9
1	4	6	3	8	2	7	9	5
3	5	8	7	9	1	4	6	2
2	7	9	6	5	4	8	3	1
4	3	2	1	6	9	5	8	7
6	9	1	8	7	5	2	4	3
5	8	7	2	4	3	9	1	6

7/1

5	7	6	8	4	1	2	9	3
3	2	4	6	5	9	8	7	1
1	9	8	3	2	7	4	6	5
6	1	9	7	8	3	5	2	4
4	8	5	9	6	2	1	3	7
2	3	7	5	1	4	9	8	6
9	6	2	1	7	5	3	4	8
7	5	3	4	9	8	6	1	2
8	4	1	2	3	6	7	5	9

7/2

3	5	4	1	7	9	8	2	6
9	7	2	8	6	5	1	4	3
8	6	1	4	2	3	9	5	7
2	4	5	9	3	1	6	7	8
6	9	8	7	5	2	4	3	1
7	1	3	6	4	8	2	9	5
1	8	7	3	9	4	5	6	2
5	3	9	2	1	6	7	8	4
4	2	6	5	8	7	3	1	9

7 / 3

7	9	3	6	1	2	5	4	8
8	2	6	4	5	9	3	7	1
4	1	5	3	8	7	2	6	9
9	6	1	7	3	5	4	8	2
2	5	4	1	9	8	7	3	6
3	7	8	2	6	4	9	1	5
6	3	9	5	7	1	8	2	4
1	8	2	9	4	3	6	5	7
5	4	7	8	2	6	1	9	3

7 / 4

4	7	9	2	5	3	8	1	6
6	2	1	8	4	7	3	9	5
8	3	5	6	9	1	4	2	7
5	4	8	3	1	2	6	7	9
1	6	2	4	7	9	5	3	8
7	9	3	5	6	8	1	4	2
9	5	6	1	2	4	7	8	3
2	8	4	7	3	5	9	6	1
3	1	7	9	8	6	2	5	4

7 / 5

5	7	8	9	4	3	1	2	6
3	4	9	6	1	2	8	5	7
1	6	2	7	5	8	9	3	4
4	2	6	3	7	1	5	8	9
9	8	5	2	6	4	7	1	3
7	3	1	8	9	5	6	4	2
2	9	3	5	8	7	4	6	1
8	1	7	4	3	6	2	9	5
6	5	4	1	2	9	3	7	8

7 / 6

3	5	9	7	2	8	1	4	6
6	4	2	5	3	1	9	7	8
1	8	7	9	4	6	3	5	2
9	6	5	8	1	2	7	3	4
2	3	4	6	9	7	5	8	1
7	1	8	3	5	4	6	2	9
4	7	1	2	6	5	8	9	3
8	9	6	4	7	3	2	1	5
5	2	3	1	8	9	4	6	7

7 / 7

9	7	4	6	5	1	8	3	2
8	1	3	9	7	2	4	6	5
2	6	5	4	8	3	9	7	1
5	8	7	1	2	4	6	9	3
6	2	9	5	3	8	7	1	4
4	3	1	7	6	9	2	5	8
3	4	6	8	1	7	5	2	9
1	5	8	2	9	6	3	4	7
7	9	2	3	4	5	1	8	6

7 / 8

5	9	7	6	1	8	4	2	3
3	2	8	9	4	5	6	7	1
1	4	6	7	3	2	9	5	8
4	5	1	8	2	6	7	3	9
7	8	3	5	9	1	2	4	6
2	6	9	3	7	4	8	1	5
6	7	5	4	8	3	1	9	2
9	3	2	1	6	7	5	8	4
8	1	4	2	5	9	3	6	7

7 / 9

2	1	5	4	7	9	3	8	6
8	6	3	5	2	1	7	4	9
4	9	7	8	3	6	2	1	5
9	4	1	3	5	8	6	2	7
5	3	2	6	1	7	8	9	4
7	8	6	9	4	2	1	5	3
1	2	9	7	6	5	4	3	8
6	5	4	2	8	3	9	7	1
3	7	8	1	9	4	5	6	2

8 / 0

5	2	8	4	1	7	6	3	9
3	7	6	5	9	8	2	4	1
4	9	1	6	2	3	5	8	7
9	4	5	1	7	6	8	2	3
2	1	3	8	4	9	7	5	6
6	8	7	2	3	5	9	1	4
7	5	4	9	8	1	3	6	2
8	3	2	7	6	4	1	9	5
1	6	9	3	5	2	4	7	8

8-1

7	4	9	3	5	2	8	1	6
3	5	1	6	8	7	2	9	4
8	2	6	1	4	9	3	7	5
9	7	3	8	2	6	4	5	1
2	6	4	5	9	1	7	8	3
1	8	5	4	7	3	6	2	9
4	3	2	9	1	8	5	6	7
6	9	8	7	3	5	1	4	2
5	1	7	2	6	4	9	3	8

8-2

7	5	3	6	9	4	1	2	8
2	9	8	7	1	3	4	5	6
1	6	4	2	8	5	9	7	3
6	4	2	5	7	8	3	1	9
9	1	5	4	3	2	8	6	7
3	8	7	1	6	9	2	4	5
8	7	1	3	4	6	5	9	2
5	3	6	9	2	1	7	8	4
4	2	9	8	5	7	6	3	1

8-3

5	1	3	9	7	8	6	4	2
4	6	2	5	3	1	8	9	7
7	8	9	2	4	6	5	1	3
6	3	8	1	2	7	9	5	4
2	4	5	6	9	3	7	8	1
9	7	1	8	5	4	2	3	6
3	9	6	7	1	5	4	2	8
8	5	4	3	6	2	1	7	9
1	2	7	4	8	9	3	6	5

8-4

2	5	4	9	1	8	7	3	6
6	8	1	3	7	2	9	5	4
9	7	3	6	4	5	2	1	8
4	1	2	8	5	9	3	6	7
5	3	6	7	2	4	8	9	1
7	9	8	1	6	3	5	4	2
1	2	5	4	3	7	6	8	9
8	4	7	5	9	6	1	2	3
3	6	9	2	8	1	4	7	5

8-5

6	4	2	1	8	7	5	9	3
7	5	1	4	3	9	6	2	8
8	3	9	5	2	6	1	4	7
1	9	4	7	6	2	3	8	5
3	6	8	9	4	5	7	1	2
2	7	5	8	1	3	4	6	9
5	8	6	3	9	4	2	7	1
9	2	3	6	7	1	8	5	4
4	1	7	2	5	8	9	3	6

8-6

1	2	8	9	5	3	6	4	7
7	6	5	2	4	8	1	3	9
4	3	9	6	7	1	2	8	5
3	4	1	5	9	2	7	6	8
6	5	7	1	8	4	3	9	2
8	9	2	3	6	7	5	1	4
2	7	4	8	1	6	9	5	3
9	1	3	4	2	5	8	7	6
5	8	6	7	3	9	4	2	1

8-7

1	5	4	9	8	6	2	3	7
7	3	9	1	4	2	6	8	5
2	6	8	7	3	5	4	1	9
4	1	7	2	6	9	8	5	3
5	9	3	8	1	4	7	6	2
6	8	2	5	7	3	9	4	1
3	2	1	4	9	8	5	7	6
8	7	5	6	2	1	3	9	4
9	4	6	3	5	7	1	2	8

8-8

6	1	7	4	5	2	3	8	9
2	8	9	3	1	6	5	4	7
4	3	5	7	9	8	6	1	2
5	6	3	9	8	7	4	2	1
8	4	1	2	6	5	9	7	3
9	7	2	1	3	4	8	5	6
1	9	8	5	2	3	7	6	4
7	2	6	8	4	9	1	3	5
3	5	4	6	7	1	2	9	8

89

3	6	4	7	1	9	2	5	8
5	7	1	2	8	4	9	3	6
2	8	9	5	3	6	1	7	4
9	3	6	1	5	7	8	4	2
7	4	2	9	6	8	3	1	5
8	1	5	3	4	2	6	9	7
1	5	8	6	7	3	4	2	9
4	9	7	8	2	1	5	6	3
6	2	3	4	9	5	7	8	1

90

3	9	6	1	2	8	4	7	5
2	5	1	6	4	7	3	8	9
4	8	7	5	3	9	2	6	1
7	2	4	8	9	6	1	5	3
9	3	8	4	5	1	6	2	7
6	1	5	2	7	3	8	9	4
5	4	3	7	8	2	9	1	6
8	6	9	3	1	5	7	4	2
1	7	2	9	6	4	5	3	8

91

5	1	6	8	4	2	7	3	9
2	4	3	7	9	1	6	8	5
8	9	7	6	5	3	4	1	2
1	8	2	5	6	9	3	4	7
6	5	4	3	7	8	9	2	1
3	7	9	1	2	4	5	6	8
4	3	8	9	1	7	2	5	6
9	6	1	2	3	5	8	7	4
7	2	5	4	8	6	1	9	3

92

7	6	9	2	5	4	3	1	8
2	1	3	7	9	8	4	6	5
4	8	5	1	6	3	9	7	2
9	4	7	3	2	6	8	5	1
3	5	6	8	1	9	7	2	4
8	2	1	4	7	5	6	9	3
5	9	8	6	4	1	2	3	7
1	3	2	9	8	7	5	4	6
6	7	4	5	3	2	1	8	9

93

5	9	4	3	2	6	1	7	8
2	1	3	7	8	5	9	6	4
6	7	8	1	9	4	3	2	5
3	4	5	2	7	1	8	9	6
9	6	2	4	5	8	7	3	1
1	8	7	6	3	9	4	5	2
4	3	9	5	1	2	6	8	7
8	2	6	9	4	7	5	1	3
7	5	1	8	6	3	2	4	9

94

9	8	1	6	4	7	3	5	2
3	5	7	1	2	9	8	6	4
4	6	2	3	5	8	1	7	9
6	7	8	4	9	1	5	2	3
5	1	4	2	3	6	9	8	7
2	9	3	7	8	5	4	1	6
8	4	6	5	7	3	2	9	1
7	3	5	9	1	2	6	4	8
1	2	9	8	6	4	7	3	5

95

4	1	5	2	8	6	3	9	7
3	9	7	4	1	5	8	2	6
6	2	8	7	9	3	5	4	1
7	6	2	3	5	9	1	8	4
8	3	4	1	7	2	9	6	5
1	5	9	8	6	4	7	3	2
9	4	1	5	2	8	6	7	3
2	7	6	9	3	1	4	5	8
5	8	3	6	4	7	2	1	9

96

1	9	5	7	4	2	3	8	6
8	2	7	5	6	3	9	1	4
3	6	4	1	8	9	5	2	7
7	1	2	6	9	5	4	3	8
6	8	9	3	1	4	2	7	5
4	5	3	8	2	7	6	9	1
2	7	1	9	5	6	8	4	3
9	3	6	4	7	8	1	5	2
5	4	8	2	3	1	7	6	9

97

8	4	2	6	3	5	1	7	9
1	9	3	4	2	7	5	8	6
7	6	5	1	8	9	4	3	2
5	3	1	9	7	4	2	6	8
9	7	4	8	6	2	3	1	5
2	8	6	3	5	1	9	4	7
6	1	9	2	4	8	7	5	3
4	5	8	7	9	3	6	2	1
3	2	7	5	1	6	8	9	4

98

4	7	9	2	8	5	3	6	1
5	6	3	9	7	1	8	2	4
1	8	2	4	3	6	5	9	7
6	3	4	7	9	2	1	8	5
7	1	8	6	5	3	9	4	2
2	9	5	8	1	4	6	7	3
9	5	7	3	2	8	4	1	6
8	4	1	5	6	7	2	3	9
3	2	6	1	4	9	7	5	8

99

3	2	7	4	5	1	6	8	9
8	5	4	6	2	9	1	3	7
1	6	9	8	7	3	2	4	5
6	7	1	3	4	5	9	2	8
9	8	5	2	1	7	3	6	4
4	3	2	9	8	6	5	7	1
5	4	6	1	3	8	7	9	2
7	9	8	5	6	2	4	1	3
2	1	3	7	9	4	8	5	6

100

3	9	5	4	8	7	6	1	2
4	2	7	9	1	6	3	5	8
8	1	6	5	2	3	7	4	9
6	8	9	3	4	5	1	2	7
2	3	1	8	7	9	4	6	5
7	5	4	2	6	1	9	8	3
9	4	3	6	5	8	2	7	1
5	7	2	1	3	4	8	9	6
1	6	8	7	9	2	5	3	4

101

9	3	8	2	6	4	5	1	7
4	2	5	8	1	7	6	3	9
6	7	1	5	9	3	8	2	4
1	6	9	4	7	2	3	5	8
2	5	3	9	8	6	4	7	1
7	8	4	3	5	1	9	6	2
3	9	7	1	4	5	2	8	6
5	4	6	7	2	8	1	9	3
8	1	2	6	3	9	7	4	5

102

2	4	3	8	9	6	1	5	7
5	9	1	7	2	3	4	6	8
7	8	6	5	1	4	9	3	2
6	5	8	9	3	7	2	4	1
4	2	7	1	8	5	3	9	6
3	1	9	6	4	2	8	7	5
9	3	5	2	7	1	6	8	4
8	6	2	4	5	9	7	1	3
1	7	4	3	6	8	5	2	9

103

6	4	3	1	5	8	9	7	2
5	7	1	2	6	9	3	4	8
2	8	9	7	4	3	1	6	5
3	6	2	9	8	4	5	1	7
4	1	8	5	7	2	6	3	9
7	9	5	3	1	6	8	2	4
9	5	6	4	2	1	7	8	3
8	2	7	6	3	5	4	9	1
1	3	4	8	9	7	2	5	6

104

5	8	4	2	7	3	6	9	1
6	1	9	8	5	4	2	3	7
7	3	2	9	6	1	4	8	5
2	6	5	4	1	9	3	7	8
4	9	1	3	8	7	5	2	6
8	7	3	6	2	5	1	4	9
3	2	8	5	9	6	7	1	4
1	4	6	7	3	8	9	5	2
9	5	7	1	4	2	8	6	3

105

2	8	9	5	1	7	4	3	6
3	5	4	6	8	2	1	9	7
6	7	1	4	3	9	2	8	5
5	2	3	8	7	1	6	4	9
8	1	7	9	6	4	5	2	3
4	9	6	2	5	3	7	1	8
7	3	8	1	4	6	9	5	2
1	6	2	3	9	5	8	7	4
9	4	5	7	2	8	3	6	1

106

5	6	7	3	2	9	1	4	8
1	8	4	6	7	5	3	9	2
2	9	3	8	1	4	7	6	5
9	5	2	1	6	7	8	3	4
4	1	8	9	5	3	2	7	6
3	7	6	2	4	8	5	1	9
8	3	5	4	9	1	6	2	7
7	2	9	5	3	6	4	8	1
6	4	1	7	8	2	9	5	3

107

5	8	2	3	1	9	4	6	7
6	1	7	5	4	8	2	9	3
3	9	4	6	7	2	8	5	1
7	4	5	9	6	3	1	8	2
9	6	3	2	8	1	5	7	4
8	2	1	7	5	4	9	3	6
1	7	8	4	9	6	3	2	5
4	3	6	8	2	5	7	1	9
2	5	9	1	3	7	6	4	8

108

7	9	4	8	6	5	3	2	1
8	3	1	9	4	2	5	6	7
2	5	6	1	7	3	9	8	4
5	6	7	3	2	1	8	4	9
1	8	3	4	9	7	2	5	6
4	2	9	5	8	6	1	7	3
9	4	2	7	3	8	6	1	5
3	1	8	6	5	4	7	9	2
6	7	5	2	1	9	4	3	8

109

4	9	6	5	7	1	2	3	8
2	5	8	4	6	3	1	9	7
7	1	3	2	9	8	5	4	6
3	8	1	9	4	2	7	6	5
5	7	4	1	3	6	9	8	2
6	2	9	8	5	7	3	1	4
9	6	2	7	1	4	8	5	3
1	4	7	3	8	5	6	2	9
8	3	5	6	2	9	4	7	1

110

3	7	9	4	8	2	1	5	6
5	8	1	6	3	7	9	4	2
6	4	2	1	9	5	8	3	7
8	3	6	2	7	9	5	1	4
1	2	5	3	4	6	7	9	8
7	9	4	5	1	8	6	2	3
4	6	7	9	2	1	3	8	5
9	5	3	8	6	4	2	7	1
2	1	8	7	5	3	4	6	9

111

8	2	9	4	1	3	5	7	6
7	1	5	9	2	6	4	8	3
3	4	6	5	8	7	2	1	9
6	7	2	3	5	4	8	9	1
4	9	8	1	7	2	3	6	5
1	5	3	8	6	9	7	2	4
5	6	4	7	9	8	1	3	2
9	3	7	2	4	1	6	5	8
2	8	1	6	3	5	9	4	7

112

3	6	4	1	7	9	5	2	8
8	1	5	3	2	4	7	6	9
2	7	9	8	5	6	3	4	1
6	8	2	4	1	7	9	5	3
7	9	1	2	3	5	4	8	6
4	5	3	6	9	8	2	1	7
9	4	8	7	6	2	1	3	5
5	3	6	9	4	1	8	7	2
1	2	7	5	8	3	6	9	4

113

1	7	3	9	5	6	8	2	4
9	5	4	7	8	2	3	6	1
2	6	8	4	3	1	9	5	7
4	8	9	5	7	3	2	1	6
7	3	1	2	6	4	5	8	9
5	2	6	1	9	8	4	7	3
3	4	5	8	1	7	6	9	2
8	1	2	6	4	9	7	3	5
6	9	7	3	2	5	1	4	8

114

5	1	2	7	8	4	3	6	9
9	7	6	2	3	5	4	1	8
8	3	4	6	1	9	2	5	7
6	2	8	1	7	3	9	4	5
1	4	9	5	2	8	6	7	3
3	5	7	4	9	6	8	2	1
2	6	3	9	5	7	1	8	4
4	9	5	8	6	1	7	3	2
7	8	1	3	4	2	5	9	6

115

5	8	4	7	2	9	6	1	3
7	3	1	8	4	6	5	2	9
6	2	9	1	5	3	8	7	4
8	4	7	9	1	2	3	6	5
1	5	6	4	3	8	2	9	7
3	9	2	6	7	5	4	8	1
9	1	5	2	6	4	7	3	8
4	6	8	3	9	7	1	5	2
2	7	3	5	8	1	9	4	6

116

1	9	7	3	2	5	6	8	4
6	3	2	8	4	7	1	9	5
5	8	4	6	1	9	3	2	7
3	7	9	4	6	2	8	5	1
2	1	8	9	5	3	7	4	6
4	6	5	7	8	1	2	3	9
7	2	6	5	3	4	9	1	8
9	4	1	2	7	8	5	6	3
8	5	3	1	9	6	4	7	2

117

3	6	9	8	7	2	1	4	5
8	5	7	3	1	4	6	9	2
2	4	1	5	9	6	8	7	3
4	3	5	9	6	1	7	2	8
6	1	8	2	3	7	4	5	9
9	7	2	4	5	8	3	6	1
7	2	3	1	4	5	9	8	6
5	9	6	7	8	3	2	1	4
1	8	4	6	2	9	5	3	7

118

3	6	9	4	7	2	5	1	8
1	4	2	9	8	5	6	7	3
7	8	5	3	1	6	9	2	4
8	9	1	5	3	4	2	6	7
4	7	3	2	6	1	8	9	5
5	2	6	8	9	7	4	3	1
2	5	7	1	4	9	3	8	6
9	1	8	6	5	3	7	4	2
6	3	4	7	2	8	1	5	9

119

2	7	3	1	9	8	4	6	5
8	4	5	2	6	3	7	9	1
6	1	9	4	5	7	8	3	2
3	8	1	7	4	5	6	2	9
5	6	4	9	8	2	1	7	3
9	2	7	3	1	6	5	8	4
7	9	6	5	3	1	2	4	8
4	5	8	6	2	9	3	1	7
1	3	2	8	7	4	9	5	6

120

4	8	2	3	7	6	1	5	9
1	5	9	4	2	8	3	7	6
3	6	7	5	1	9	4	8	2
2	9	6	8	3	1	7	4	5
8	4	5	7	6	2	9	3	1
7	1	3	9	4	5	6	2	8
6	2	4	1	5	3	8	9	7
9	3	1	2	8	7	5	6	4
5	7	8	6	9	4	2	1	3

1 2 1

7	8	3	4	1	9	6	2	5
9	1	4	6	2	5	8	7	3
6	2	5	7	3	8	4	9	1
8	9	6	5	7	1	3	4	2
2	4	7	8	6	3	5	1	9
3	5	1	9	4	2	7	8	6
1	3	8	2	5	4	9	6	7
5	6	9	1	8	7	2	3	4
4	7	2	3	9	6	1	5	8

1 2 2

9	4	3	5	1	7	2	6	8
2	6	8	3	9	4	7	1	5
7	5	1	2	8	6	4	9	3
6	3	9	8	4	2	5	7	1
1	8	4	6	7	5	3	2	9
5	7	2	9	3	1	6	8	4
4	1	5	7	6	9	8	3	2
3	2	6	1	5	8	9	4	7
8	9	7	4	2	3	1	5	6

1 2 3

7	5	8	9	2	1	6	3	4
1	3	4	7	5	6	8	9	2
6	9	2	4	8	3	5	7	1
3	1	6	2	4	9	7	5	8
8	4	5	6	3	7	1	2	9
2	7	9	8	1	5	4	6	3
4	6	7	1	9	2	3	8	5
9	8	3	5	7	4	2	1	6
5	2	1	3	6	8	9	4	7

1 2 4

9	3	4	5	8	6	1	7	2
7	2	5	1	3	4	8	9	6
8	6	1	7	9	2	4	5	3
6	4	3	2	5	9	7	8	1
5	7	8	6	1	3	2	4	9
1	9	2	8	4	7	3	6	5
4	5	9	3	7	1	6	2	8
3	8	6	4	2	5	9	1	7
2	1	7	9	6	8	5	3	4

1 2 5

5	8	3	2	7	1	9	4	6
7	6	2	4	9	3	1	5	8
4	9	1	8	6	5	7	3	2
3	2	6	7	4	8	5	1	9
9	7	4	1	5	6	2	8	3
1	5	8	9	3	2	4	6	7
8	4	9	6	1	7	3	2	5
2	1	5	3	8	9	6	7	4
6	3	7	5	2	4	8	9	1

1 2 6

4	2	1	3	6	7	5	9	8
5	9	8	1	2	4	3	6	7
7	3	6	9	5	8	2	1	4
2	6	9	7	4	1	8	5	3
3	7	4	5	8	6	9	2	1
1	8	5	2	9	3	7	4	6
6	4	2	8	7	5	1	3	9
9	1	7	6	3	2	4	8	5
8	5	3	4	1	9	6	7	2

1 2 7

7	3	8	9	6	1	5	2	4
1	5	6	4	2	7	9	3	8
4	9	2	8	5	3	1	7	6
9	2	1	6	7	8	4	5	3
3	8	7	5	4	9	2	6	1
5	6	4	3	1	2	7	8	9
2	7	9	1	8	6	3	4	5
8	4	3	7	9	5	6	1	2
6	1	5	2	3	4	8	9	7

1 2 8

9	5	2	3	1	4	7	6	8
6	3	1	9	7	8	4	2	5
8	7	4	2	5	6	9	1	3
4	6	8	7	2	9	5	3	1
7	2	3	5	4	1	6	8	9
5	1	9	6	8	3	2	7	4
1	4	6	8	9	2	3	5	7
2	9	5	1	3	7	8	4	6
3	8	7	4	6	5	1	9	2

129

8	5	1	7	4	9	2	3	6
4	2	7	5	3	6	8	9	1
9	3	6	2	8	1	4	5	7
3	1	4	9	6	8	5	7	2
2	9	5	3	7	4	6	1	8
7	6	8	1	5	2	9	4	3
6	7	2	4	1	5	3	8	9
1	4	9	8	2	3	7	6	5
5	8	3	6	9	7	1	2	4

130

4	8	5	1	9	7	3	2	6
9	1	7	3	6	2	4	8	5
3	6	2	4	8	5	9	7	1
1	2	6	9	4	8	5	3	7
7	4	3	5	2	1	6	9	8
8	5	9	6	7	3	2	1	4
5	7	4	2	1	9	8	6	3
2	3	1	8	5	6	7	4	9
6	9	8	7	3	4	1	5	2

131

6	8	4	1	9	3	7	5	2
2	1	5	7	8	4	3	6	9
3	7	9	6	2	5	4	1	8
9	3	1	8	7	6	5	2	4
5	6	2	4	3	1	8	9	7
8	4	7	9	5	2	6	3	1
4	2	8	3	6	9	1	7	5
1	5	3	2	4	7	9	8	6
7	9	6	5	1	8	2	4	3

132

6	7	1	5	9	2	8	4	3
2	3	8	4	6	1	7	9	5
5	9	4	3	8	7	2	6	1
4	8	2	6	7	5	1	3	9
3	1	9	8	2	4	6	5	7
7	5	6	9	1	3	4	2	8
9	4	7	1	3	6	5	8	2
1	6	3	2	5	8	9	7	4
8	2	5	7	4	9	3	1	6

133

4	1	5	2	3	8	9	7	6
7	6	8	9	1	4	2	3	5
3	9	2	7	5	6	4	1	8
9	5	1	8	6	3	7	4	2
8	3	6	4	7	2	5	9	1
2	7	4	5	9	1	6	8	3
1	2	7	3	4	5	8	6	9
6	8	9	1	2	7	3	5	4
5	4	3	6	8	9	1	2	7

134

9	8	3	7	6	1	4	5	2
4	7	5	2	3	9	8	1	6
1	6	2	5	4	8	3	7	9
6	9	8	3	1	4	5	2	7
3	1	7	6	2	5	9	8	4
2	5	4	8	9	7	6	3	1
5	2	6	4	7	3	1	9	8
8	4	9	1	5	2	7	6	3
7	3	1	9	8	6	2	4	5

135

5	8	3	7	9	4	2	1	6
2	1	9	6	3	5	8	4	7
4	6	7	2	8	1	3	9	5
9	2	4	5	7	8	1	6	3
1	5	6	4	2	3	7	8	9
3	7	8	9	1	6	4	5	2
6	3	2	1	4	9	5	7	8
7	9	1	8	5	2	6	3	4
8	4	5	3	6	7	9	2	1

136

3	9	8	2	5	1	6	4	7
2	5	4	8	6	7	9	3	1
6	7	1	9	4	3	2	5	8
9	1	7	3	2	5	4	8	6
5	2	6	1	8	4	3	7	9
8	4	3	7	9	6	1	2	5
4	6	9	5	3	8	7	1	2
7	8	2	4	1	9	5	6	3
1	3	5	6	7	2	8	9	4

137

1	7	9	3	6	4	2	8	5
5	3	4	2	1	8	7	6	9
2	6	8	7	9	5	4	3	1
7	2	1	5	3	9	6	4	8
8	9	5	4	7	6	3	1	2
6	4	3	1	8	2	5	9	7
4	8	7	9	5	3	1	2	6
3	5	6	8	2	1	9	7	4
9	1	2	6	4	7	8	5	3

138

9	2	1	5	4	8	6	7	3
4	7	5	9	6	3	2	1	8
6	3	8	1	2	7	9	5	4
1	4	9	8	3	6	5	2	7
7	5	3	4	9	2	8	6	1
2	8	6	7	5	1	3	4	9
8	6	2	3	7	4	1	9	5
3	9	4	2	1	5	7	8	6
5	1	7	6	8	9	4	3	2

139

8	4	3	2	1	5	9	6	7
1	7	6	8	9	4	5	2	3
9	5	2	3	6	7	4	1	8
3	2	4	1	5	6	8	7	9
7	8	1	9	2	3	6	4	5
5	6	9	7	4	8	1	3	2
2	3	5	4	8	1	7	9	6
6	1	7	5	3	9	2	8	4
4	9	8	6	7	2	3	5	1

140

2	3	7	4	1	8	9	5	6
8	4	1	6	9	5	2	3	7
6	9	5	7	3	2	4	1	8
4	5	9	3	2	7	6	8	1
7	2	3	1	8	6	5	4	9
1	6	8	5	4	9	3	7	2
9	8	4	2	7	3	1	6	5
3	7	6	9	5	1	8	2	4
5	1	2	8	6	4	7	9	3

141

1	5	8	7	4	9	6	2	3
9	2	6	8	5	3	7	4	1
4	7	3	2	1	6	5	8	9
5	1	4	3	7	8	9	6	2
3	8	9	6	2	5	4	1	7
7	6	2	4	9	1	8	3	5
6	9	1	5	8	2	3	7	4
8	4	5	1	3	7	2	9	6
2	3	7	9	6	4	1	5	8

142

6	9	5	3	1	2	4	8	7
2	1	3	4	7	8	5	9	6
4	7	8	9	6	5	1	2	3
3	8	7	5	2	9	6	1	4
1	5	4	8	3	6	9	7	2
9	6	2	1	4	7	8	3	5
7	2	9	6	5	1	3	4	8
8	4	6	7	9	3	2	5	1
5	3	1	2	8	4	7	6	9

143

7	3	6	4	2	1	9	5	8
1	2	5	9	8	7	6	4	3
8	9	4	3	5	6	7	1	2
3	8	7	5	6	2	4	9	1
4	5	9	1	7	3	2	8	6
6	1	2	8	4	9	3	7	5
5	6	3	7	9	8	1	2	4
2	7	8	6	1	4	5	3	9
9	4	1	2	3	5	8	6	7

144

8	5	7	3	6	2	4	9	1
4	6	3	8	1	9	7	5	2
1	2	9	7	5	4	3	6	8
2	7	1	5	8	3	9	4	6
9	3	8	4	2	6	1	7	5
5	4	6	1	9	7	2	8	3
6	9	5	2	4	1	8	3	7
3	8	2	9	7	5	6	1	4
7	1	4	6	3	8	5	2	9

145

9	7	5	1	2	6	8	4	3
2	6	3	8	4	7	9	5	1
1	4	8	3	9	5	2	6	7
6	3	4	7	8	2	5	1	9
7	8	9	5	1	4	6	3	2
5	1	2	6	3	9	4	7	8
8	9	1	4	5	3	7	2	6
3	5	6	2	7	8	1	9	4
4	2	7	9	6	1	3	8	5

146

7	8	5	9	3	2	1	6	4
6	2	9	7	1	4	3	8	5
3	1	4	6	8	5	2	7	9
1	3	7	8	9	6	5	4	2
2	9	8	5	4	7	6	1	3
5	4	6	1	2	3	8	9	7
8	5	3	4	6	9	7	2	1
4	7	1	2	5	8	9	3	6
9	6	2	3	7	1	4	5	8

147

3	9	4	5	7	2	1	6	8
7	1	5	4	8	6	3	9	2
2	6	8	3	1	9	7	5	4
5	2	1	7	4	8	6	3	9
6	8	9	1	2	3	5	4	7
4	3	7	6	9	5	2	8	1
9	7	6	2	5	4	8	1	3
8	5	2	9	3	1	4	7	6
1	4	3	8	6	7	9	2	5

148

1	7	5	9	4	3	2	8	6
9	6	8	1	7	2	3	4	5
3	2	4	8	5	6	7	9	1
4	1	7	2	6	9	5	3	8
5	3	6	7	8	4	1	2	9
8	9	2	5	3	1	4	6	7
2	5	3	6	9	7	8	1	4
6	8	1	4	2	5	9	7	3
7	4	9	3	1	8	6	5	2

149

9	4	8	5	7	2	1	3	6
2	5	7	6	1	3	4	9	8
3	6	1	4	9	8	7	2	5
4	3	2	8	6	1	5	7	9
1	9	6	3	5	7	2	8	4
8	7	5	2	4	9	3	6	1
7	1	3	9	8	4	6	5	2
5	8	4	7	2	6	9	1	3
6	2	9	1	3	5	8	4	7

150

1	5	4	3	2	6	8	7	9
3	2	6	9	8	7	1	5	4
9	8	7	4	5	1	2	3	6
5	3	2	6	7	9	4	8	1
7	4	8	2	1	5	6	9	3
6	9	1	8	3	4	5	2	7
8	6	5	1	9	3	7	4	2
4	7	3	5	6	2	9	1	8
2	1	9	7	4	8	3	6	5

151

9	3	1	4	2	7	5	8	6
5	7	8	1	9	6	2	3	4
2	6	4	8	5	3	7	1	9
7	9	5	2	8	4	3	6	1
1	4	6	5	3	9	8	2	7
8	2	3	7	6	1	9	4	5
4	8	7	3	1	5	6	9	2
3	1	9	6	7	2	4	5	8
6	5	2	9	4	8	1	7	3

152

3	6	1	2	9	8	5	4	7
8	7	5	4	3	1	6	9	2
4	2	9	6	5	7	3	1	8
6	4	3	9	1	2	8	7	5
1	9	7	8	6	5	4	2	3
2	5	8	7	4	3	9	6	1
7	3	6	5	2	9	1	8	4
9	1	2	3	8	4	7	5	6
5	8	4	1	7	6	2	3	9

153

7	1	6	5	3	9	8	2	4
2	9	8	7	4	6	3	1	5
3	5	4	1	8	2	9	7	6
6	7	3	4	1	8	2	5	9
9	8	2	3	6	5	7	4	1
1	4	5	9	2	7	6	8	3
8	6	9	2	5	4	1	3	7
4	3	7	8	9	1	5	6	2
5	2	1	6	7	3	4	9	8

154

8	3	9	1	4	7	5	6	2
6	1	4	3	5	2	9	8	7
5	7	2	6	9	8	1	4	3
9	6	5	8	7	3	4	2	1
1	4	7	9	2	5	6	3	8
3	2	8	4	1	6	7	5	9
7	9	3	2	6	4	8	1	5
2	5	6	7	8	1	3	9	4
4	8	1	5	3	9	2	7	6

155

2	1	3	9	7	4	6	8	5
6	4	8	5	1	2	7	9	3
9	5	7	3	6	8	1	2	4
1	9	4	8	5	7	3	6	2
8	3	6	2	4	9	5	7	1
5	7	2	1	3	6	8	4	9
4	2	5	7	8	3	9	1	6
7	6	1	4	9	5	2	3	8
3	8	9	6	2	1	4	5	7

156

9	8	4	2	7	3	1	6	5
2	1	6	4	8	5	9	3	7
5	7	3	6	9	1	4	8	2
3	6	2	1	5	4	8	7	9
7	4	9	8	6	2	5	1	3
1	5	8	7	3	9	2	4	6
8	3	1	5	2	7	6	9	4
6	9	5	3	4	8	7	2	1
4	2	7	9	1	6	3	5	8

157

8	3	4	9	7	6	2	1	5
5	9	2	8	1	4	3	7	6
6	7	1	2	3	5	4	9	8
1	6	9	7	4	3	8	5	2
3	4	5	1	8	2	9	6	7
7	2	8	6	5	9	1	3	4
9	1	7	4	6	8	5	2	3
4	5	6	3	2	1	7	8	9
2	8	3	5	9	7	6	4	1

158

2	3	5	6	1	4	8	9	7
7	6	1	8	9	2	3	4	5
8	9	4	5	7	3	1	2	6
1	7	3	4	8	6	9	5	2
9	5	6	3	2	1	4	7	8
4	2	8	7	5	9	6	1	3
5	8	9	1	6	7	2	3	4
6	4	2	9	3	5	7	8	1
3	1	7	2	4	8	5	6	9

159

1	5	2	8	9	3	7	4	6
4	7	6	2	5	1	9	8	3
9	8	3	7	4	6	1	5	2
7	1	5	6	8	2	3	9	4
2	9	4	1	3	5	8	6	7
6	3	8	4	7	9	5	2	1
5	6	1	9	2	7	4	3	8
8	2	9	3	1	4	6	7	5
3	4	7	5	6	8	2	1	9

160

3	7	6	9	8	5	4	1	2
8	5	9	4	1	2	6	3	7
1	2	4	3	6	7	5	9	8
5	1	8	7	3	4	9	2	6
7	6	3	1	2	9	8	4	5
4	9	2	6	5	8	1	7	3
2	3	1	8	9	6	7	5	4
9	8	7	5	4	3	2	6	1
6	4	5	2	7	1	3	8	9

161

5	3	8	2	9	7	1	4	6
9	6	4	8	3	1	7	2	5
1	2	7	6	4	5	9	8	3
2	8	6	7	1	3	5	9	4
3	9	1	5	6	4	2	7	8
4	7	5	9	2	8	3	6	1
7	4	2	3	5	6	8	1	9
8	1	3	4	7	9	6	5	2
6	5	9	1	8	2	4	3	7

162

6	8	4	5	9	3	1	2	7
7	9	3	4	2	1	5	8	6
5	1	2	6	7	8	3	4	9
2	5	6	3	8	9	4	7	1
3	4	1	2	6	7	9	5	8
9	7	8	1	5	4	2	6	3
8	3	7	9	4	2	6	1	5
4	6	9	8	1	5	7	3	2
1	2	5	7	3	6	8	9	4

163

7	6	8	4	1	3	9	5	2
3	4	2	6	5	9	1	7	8
9	5	1	8	2	7	6	3	4
5	8	6	9	4	2	3	1	7
1	3	4	7	8	6	2	9	5
2	7	9	5	3	1	4	8	6
4	1	7	3	6	8	5	2	9
6	9	3	2	7	5	8	4	1
8	2	5	1	9	4	7	6	3

164

9	1	5	7	3	4	6	8	2
7	4	8	5	2	6	1	3	9
2	3	6	1	9	8	5	7	4
4	5	3	9	8	2	7	1	6
1	6	2	3	5	7	9	4	8
8	7	9	6	4	1	3	2	5
5	8	1	2	6	3	4	9	7
3	9	4	8	7	5	2	6	1
6	2	7	4	1	9	8	5	3

165

5	7	6	2	9	8	1	4	3
3	2	1	6	5	4	8	7	9
9	4	8	3	7	1	2	5	6
2	9	4	5	8	7	3	6	1
8	6	5	1	3	9	7	2	4
1	3	7	4	6	2	9	8	5
7	1	2	9	4	5	6	3	8
4	8	3	7	1	6	5	9	2
6	5	9	8	2	3	4	1	7

166

3	5	1	9	6	2	7	4	8
6	9	4	8	7	1	3	5	2
8	7	2	5	4	3	1	6	9
4	8	3	7	2	5	6	9	1
2	6	5	1	3	9	4	8	7
9	1	7	4	8	6	2	3	5
5	2	9	3	1	4	8	7	6
7	3	6	2	9	8	5	1	4
1	4	8	6	5	7	9	2	3

167

2	5	6	8	9	7	4	1	3
8	4	3	1	5	6	2	9	7
9	1	7	3	4	2	6	5	8
5	8	4	2	6	9	7	3	1
1	7	9	4	8	3	5	2	6
3	6	2	7	1	5	9	8	4
6	3	1	9	2	4	8	7	5
7	2	5	6	3	8	1	4	9
4	9	8	5	7	1	3	6	2

168

7	1	9	4	2	3	8	5	6
6	4	2	5	1	8	9	3	7
3	8	5	6	7	9	2	1	4
8	7	3	2	5	6	1	4	9
5	9	6	8	4	1	7	2	3
4	2	1	3	9	7	5	6	8
1	6	8	7	3	5	4	9	2
2	5	7	9	6	4	3	8	1
9	3	4	1	8	2	6	7	5

169

9	2	4	5	1	6	8	7	3
1	6	5	7	3	8	4	2	9
8	7	3	4	9	2	5	6	1
4	9	7	6	8	3	1	5	2
3	1	6	9	2	5	7	4	8
5	8	2	1	4	7	3	9	6
6	3	9	8	7	4	2	1	5
7	5	8	2	6	1	9	3	4
2	4	1	3	5	9	6	8	7

170

2	6	9	5	1	3	4	8	7
8	3	5	4	2	7	1	6	9
7	1	4	9	6	8	3	2	5
9	5	2	3	7	4	8	1	6
3	8	6	1	5	2	9	7	4
4	7	1	6	8	9	5	3	2
5	2	3	8	9	6	7	4	1
1	4	7	2	3	5	6	9	8
6	9	8	7	4	1	2	5	3

171

1	6	5	7	3	9	2	4	8
7	4	8	5	1	2	9	6	3
3	2	9	4	6	8	1	7	5
4	9	3	8	7	6	5	2	1
2	5	7	9	4	1	8	3	6
8	1	6	2	5	3	4	9	7
9	8	1	6	2	7	3	5	4
5	7	2	3	8	4	6	1	9
6	3	4	1	9	5	7	8	2

172

9	1	6	4	5	2	7	3	8
7	4	2	3	6	8	9	1	5
8	3	5	9	7	1	6	4	2
1	8	7	2	4	6	5	9	3
2	5	9	7	1	3	4	8	6
4	6	3	5	8	9	2	7	1
3	9	8	6	2	7	1	5	4
5	2	1	8	9	4	3	6	7
6	7	4	1	3	5	8	2	9

173

6	3	5	4	1	9	7	2	8
2	7	1	6	5	8	3	4	9
8	9	4	7	3	2	5	1	6
1	6	2	9	8	3	4	7	5
3	8	9	5	7	4	1	6	2
4	5	7	2	6	1	9	8	3
7	2	6	1	9	5	8	3	4
5	1	8	3	4	6	2	9	7
9	4	3	8	2	7	6	5	1

174

2	7	8	3	9	5	1	4	6
1	6	4	8	2	7	3	5	9
5	3	9	4	1	6	7	2	8
8	5	6	1	3	9	2	7	4
7	4	2	6	5	8	9	1	3
9	1	3	7	4	2	8	6	5
6	9	7	5	8	1	4	3	2
3	2	1	9	6	4	5	8	7
4	8	5	2	7	3	6	9	1

175

1	3	7	6	4	8	9	2	5
9	4	2	7	5	3	1	6	8
6	8	5	9	2	1	4	3	7
8	2	1	4	9	7	6	5	3
7	5	6	3	1	2	8	9	4
3	9	4	5	8	6	7	1	2
2	1	9	8	3	4	5	7	6
5	7	8	2	6	9	3	4	1
4	6	3	1	7	5	2	8	9

176

9	3	1	7	2	5	6	8	4
7	5	2	4	6	8	1	3	9
8	6	4	1	3	9	5	7	2
5	4	7	9	1	3	8	2	6
2	1	6	5	8	7	9	4	3
3	9	8	2	4	6	7	1	5
6	8	5	3	7	4	2	9	1
4	2	9	8	5	1	3	6	7
1	7	3	6	9	2	4	5	8

177

2	3	1	8	4	5	6	9	7
7	6	9	2	1	3	5	8	4
5	8	4	9	7	6	2	3	1
6	9	2	7	5	1	8	4	3
8	5	3	4	2	9	7	1	6
1	4	7	3	6	8	9	5	2
4	1	8	6	9	7	3	2	5
3	2	6	5	8	4	1	7	9
9	7	5	1	3	2	4	6	8

178

5	2	6	8	9	3	1	7	4
4	7	9	1	2	6	8	3	5
1	8	3	5	4	7	6	2	9
9	5	4	7	3	8	2	6	1
3	1	2	4	6	5	9	8	7
7	6	8	2	1	9	4	5	3
2	3	5	9	8	1	7	4	6
8	9	7	6	5	4	3	1	2
6	4	1	3	7	2	5	9	8

179

2	6	7	4	9	1	5	8	3
4	1	5	3	8	7	6	9	2
8	9	3	2	6	5	7	4	1
9	8	2	7	3	6	1	5	4
3	5	4	1	2	9	8	6	7
1	7	6	5	4	8	3	2	9
7	4	1	8	5	2	9	3	6
5	3	9	6	7	4	2	1	8
6	2	8	9	1	3	4	7	5

180

2	4	8	3	6	1	9	7	5
1	3	9	2	7	5	8	4	6
6	7	5	9	4	8	3	2	1
5	9	4	1	8	6	7	3	2
3	2	1	5	9	7	4	6	8
8	6	7	4	2	3	1	5	9
4	8	3	6	1	2	5	9	7
7	5	2	8	3	9	6	1	4
9	1	6	7	5	4	2	8	3

181

1	8	3	6	2	7	5	9	4
2	6	7	5	4	9	1	3	8
9	5	4	3	8	1	6	7	2
8	2	6	4	5	3	7	1	9
3	1	5	9	7	2	4	8	6
7	4	9	1	6	8	3	2	5
5	3	1	2	9	4	8	6	7
4	7	2	8	1	6	9	5	3
6	9	8	7	3	5	2	4	1

182

3	5	4	2	8	9	1	7	6
9	2	8	1	7	6	5	4	3
7	6	1	4	5	3	8	2	9
2	4	5	7	6	1	3	9	8
1	7	9	5	3	8	4	6	2
8	3	6	9	2	4	7	5	1
6	1	2	8	4	7	9	3	5
4	9	3	6	1	5	2	8	7
5	8	7	3	9	2	6	1	4

183

9	6	7	3	1	4	2	5	8
5	2	8	9	6	7	4	3	1
3	4	1	8	2	5	7	6	9
6	7	9	1	4	3	8	2	5
4	1	2	5	8	6	3	9	7
8	5	3	7	9	2	1	4	6
1	8	4	2	5	9	6	7	3
7	9	6	4	3	1	5	8	2
2	3	5	6	7	8	9	1	4

184

6	1	3	5	9	7	8	2	4
2	8	7	3	4	6	5	1	9
4	9	5	8	2	1	6	7	3
7	6	2	1	5	3	9	4	8
8	5	4	9	6	2	7	3	1
9	3	1	4	7	8	2	6	5
1	2	8	7	3	9	4	5	6
3	4	6	2	8	5	1	9	7
5	7	9	6	1	4	3	8	2

8	1	5	6	9	7	2	3	4
9	4	3	2	5	1	6	8	7
2	7	6	4	8	3	1	9	5
5	3	8	9	1	2	7	4	6
4	6	7	8	3	5	9	1	2
1	2	9	7	4	6	3	5	8
6	9	4	1	2	8	5	7	3
7	5	1	3	6	4	8	2	9
3	8	2	5	7	9	4	6	1

6	8	3	2	4	7	5	9	1
2	7	1	8	5	9	3	6	4
5	4	9	1	3	6	8	2	7
7	1	4	6	8	5	9	3	2
9	6	2	7	1	3	4	8	5
3	5	8	9	2	4	1	7	6
1	3	6	4	9	2	7	5	8
4	2	5	3	7	8	6	1	9
8	9	7	5	6	1	2	4	3

9	6	3	4	2	7	8	5	1
1	4	7	6	5	8	2	9	3
8	5	2	3	9	1	7	6	4
6	8	1	7	3	9	5	4	2
3	2	4	5	1	6	9	7	8
7	9	5	2	8	4	1	3	6
5	7	6	8	4	2	3	1	9
2	3	9	1	6	5	4	8	7
4	1	8	9	7	3	6	2	5

3	1	9	5	4	8	6	7	2
5	4	6	1	7	2	3	9	8
7	2	8	6	3	9	4	5	1
6	3	2	9	5	1	8	4	7
1	5	7	8	2	4	9	3	6
9	8	4	3	6	7	2	1	5
4	6	5	2	1	3	7	8	9
8	7	1	4	9	6	5	2	3
2	9	3	7	8	5	1	6	4

9	6	7	3	1	4	5	2	8
8	3	4	2	9	5	6	7	1
5	1	2	6	8	7	3	9	4
1	7	5	8	6	3	2	4	9
2	9	3	4	7	1	8	5	6
6	4	8	9	5	2	1	3	7
7	8	9	5	2	6	4	1	3
3	5	6	1	4	9	7	8	2
4	2	1	7	3	8	9	6	5

7	1	4	9	6	5	2	8	3
3	6	8	1	2	4	5	7	9
2	9	5	3	8	7	6	4	1
1	5	3	6	4	9	7	2	8
6	2	9	8	7	1	3	5	4
4	8	7	5	3	2	1	9	6
8	4	2	7	1	6	9	3	5
5	7	6	4	9	3	8	1	2
9	3	1	2	5	8	4	6	7

7	1	3	4	5	8	2	6	9
9	8	5	2	6	3	1	4	7
2	4	6	7	1	9	5	8	3
5	2	8	6	7	4	3	9	1
3	6	7	9	2	1	4	5	8
1	9	4	3	8	5	6	7	2
8	3	2	5	9	6	7	1	4
4	5	9	1	3	7	8	2	6
6	7	1	8	4	2	9	3	5

2	6	7	8	9	3	4	1	5
1	8	4	6	7	5	2	9	3
5	9	3	2	1	4	8	6	7
3	1	6	9	4	7	5	2	8
7	2	5	1	3	8	9	4	6
9	4	8	5	6	2	7	3	1
8	3	2	4	5	6	1	7	9
4	7	9	3	8	1	6	5	2
6	5	1	7	2	9	3	8	4

193

5	4	8	9	2	3	6	7	1
1	9	7	4	5	6	8	3	2
2	6	3	8	7	1	9	4	5
6	7	5	2	4	8	3	1	9
8	1	9	7	3	5	4	2	6
4	3	2	6	1	9	5	8	7
7	5	6	1	8	4	2	9	3
9	2	4	3	6	7	1	5	8
3	8	1	5	9	2	7	6	4

194

8	4	9	1	3	5	2	6	7
2	6	7	4	9	8	3	5	1
1	5	3	2	7	6	4	9	8
4	2	8	6	5	3	1	7	9
9	3	6	8	1	7	5	4	2
5	7	1	9	4	2	6	8	3
6	8	5	3	2	9	7	1	4
7	1	2	5	8	4	9	3	6
3	9	4	7	6	1	8	2	5

195

2	3	6	1	9	8	4	7	5
1	8	9	4	5	7	6	3	2
7	4	5	3	2	6	9	1	8
9	7	3	2	1	5	8	6	4
4	2	8	6	3	9	1	5	7
6	5	1	8	7	4	2	9	3
8	1	7	9	4	3	5	2	6
5	6	2	7	8	1	3	4	9
3	9	4	5	6	2	7	8	1

196

2	7	5	4	3	9	6	1	8
6	3	8	1	5	2	7	4	9
4	9	1	7	6	8	5	3	2
7	4	3	9	2	5	1	8	6
8	1	2	3	4	6	9	7	5
9	5	6	8	1	7	4	2	3
1	6	4	5	8	3	2	9	7
5	8	7	2	9	4	3	6	1
3	2	9	6	7	1	8	5	4

197

1	8	6	2	7	3	4	5	9
9	2	3	8	4	5	6	7	1
4	5	7	6	1	9	8	3	2
6	4	5	3	9	8	1	2	7
3	7	8	1	5	2	9	6	4
2	1	9	7	6	4	5	8	3
8	6	2	4	3	1	7	9	5
7	9	4	5	2	6	3	1	8
5	3	1	9	8	7	2	4	6

198

7	3	1	4	2	8	5	6	9
9	2	5	3	6	7	1	4	8
8	4	6	1	5	9	7	2	3
3	8	9	2	1	6	4	5	7
6	1	4	7	3	5	9	8	2
5	7	2	8	9	4	3	1	6
1	6	8	9	4	3	2	7	5
2	5	3	6	7	1	8	9	4
4	9	7	5	8	2	6	3	1

199

2	5	4	1	9	7	6	3	8
1	7	8	5	6	3	2	4	9
6	3	9	8	4	2	1	7	5
7	2	1	9	3	5	8	6	4
8	4	6	2	7	1	5	9	3
3	9	5	6	8	4	7	1	2
4	6	2	3	1	8	9	5	7
9	8	7	4	5	6	3	2	1
5	1	3	7	2	9	4	8	6

200

7	3	6	5	1	4	9	8	2
8	5	2	3	6	9	4	1	7
4	9	1	7	2	8	5	6	3
2	1	3	4	7	5	6	9	8
5	8	9	2	3	6	1	7	4
6	7	4	8	9	1	3	2	5
3	6	5	9	8	7	2	4	1
9	4	8	1	5	2	7	3	6
1	2	7	6	4	3	8	5	9

201

2	4	1	7	9	3	8	5	6
3	5	9	6	8	4	2	7	1
7	8	6	1	2	5	3	9	4
6	1	2	5	4	8	9	3	7
8	3	5	9	7	1	6	4	2
9	7	4	3	6	2	5	1	8
5	9	7	8	1	6	4	2	3
1	2	8	4	3	9	7	6	5
4	6	3	2	5	7	1	8	9

202

6	4	3	9	1	7	8	2	5
1	5	2	4	3	8	7	6	9
7	8	9	5	6	2	4	1	3
5	1	6	3	8	9	2	4	7
3	9	8	2	7	4	6	5	1
4	2	7	6	5	1	3	9	8
9	7	5	8	2	6	1	3	4
8	6	4	1	9	3	5	7	2
2	3	1	7	4	5	9	8	6

203

3	1	2	9	4	7	5	8	6
9	7	8	3	6	5	1	2	4
5	4	6	2	8	1	3	7	9
8	2	5	6	3	4	9	1	7
1	6	7	8	5	9	2	4	3
4	3	9	1	7	2	8	6	5
6	9	3	7	2	8	4	5	1
2	5	1	4	9	6	7	3	8
7	8	4	5	1	3	6	9	2

204

7	3	9	5	4	8	1	2	6
2	8	6	9	1	3	7	5	4
4	1	5	7	6	2	8	3	9
8	6	3	2	7	4	5	9	1
1	4	2	8	5	9	6	7	3
5	9	7	6	3	1	2	4	8
6	2	4	3	8	5	9	1	7
9	7	1	4	2	6	3	8	5
3	5	8	1	9	7	4	6	2

205

7	9	1	2	3	6	8	4	5
6	4	3	8	9	5	1	7	2
2	5	8	7	1	4	6	9	3
8	6	9	4	5	2	7	3	1
3	7	2	9	6	1	4	5	8
5	1	4	3	7	8	2	6	9
4	3	7	1	8	9	5	2	6
1	2	6	5	4	3	9	8	7
9	8	5	6	2	7	3	1	4

206

2	4	6	7	9	1	8	5	3
5	8	1	3	2	4	9	6	7
9	7	3	5	8	6	4	1	2
8	9	4	6	3	2	1	7	5
6	1	5	8	4	7	3	2	9
7	3	2	1	5	9	6	8	4
4	6	8	2	7	3	5	9	1
1	2	9	4	6	5	7	3	8
3	5	7	9	1	8	2	4	6

207

2	7	5	8	3	1	9	4	6
3	1	8	6	9	4	5	7	2
9	4	6	2	7	5	1	3	8
1	6	3	7	8	2	4	9	5
7	8	2	4	5	9	3	6	1
5	9	4	3	1	6	2	8	7
4	5	7	9	2	8	6	1	3
8	2	9	1	6	3	7	5	4
6	3	1	5	4	7	8	2	9

208

7	3	4	1	6	9	2	8	5
2	5	8	7	3	4	9	1	6
9	1	6	5	2	8	7	3	4
3	8	9	6	1	7	5	4	2
4	2	1	8	9	5	6	7	3
6	7	5	3	4	2	1	9	8
5	6	3	4	7	1	8	2	9
8	9	7	2	5	3	4	6	1
1	4	2	9	8	6	3	5	7

209

6	9	7	2	3	8	5	4	1
1	2	8	5	4	6	9	7	3
4	5	3	1	9	7	6	8	2
2	3	4	8	5	9	7	1	6
5	6	1	4	7	2	3	9	8
7	8	9	6	1	3	4	2	5
9	4	5	3	8	1	2	6	7
8	7	6	9	2	5	1	3	4
3	1	2	7	6	4	8	5	9

210

2	7	8	9	4	5	1	3	6
4	6	9	1	3	8	5	2	7
1	5	3	2	6	7	4	8	9
8	3	2	7	1	6	9	4	5
5	9	7	4	8	3	6	1	2
6	1	4	5	2	9	3	7	8
7	4	6	8	9	1	2	5	3
9	2	5	3	7	4	8	6	1
3	8	1	6	5	2	7	9	4

211

2	7	3	6	5	8	9	4	1
9	5	6	4	1	2	7	8	3
4	8	1	7	9	3	2	6	5
3	6	9	2	8	5	1	7	4
7	1	8	9	6	4	3	5	2
5	2	4	1	3	7	6	9	8
1	9	2	8	4	6	5	3	7
8	3	7	5	2	9	4	1	6
6	4	5	3	7	1	8	2	9

212

6	9	7	1	3	5	8	2	4
2	5	8	6	4	7	9	3	1
1	3	4	9	8	2	7	6	5
3	8	1	5	7	4	6	9	2
9	7	2	3	1	6	4	5	8
4	6	5	2	9	8	1	7	3
8	1	6	7	2	3	5	4	9
7	2	9	4	5	1	3	8	6
5	4	3	8	6	9	2	1	7

213

8	6	4	1	3	5	2	9	7
9	7	1	2	6	8	4	5	3
5	2	3	4	7	9	8	6	1
7	1	2	5	8	6	9	3	4
3	9	8	7	4	2	6	1	5
6	4	5	9	1	3	7	8	2
1	5	9	6	2	4	3	7	8
2	8	6	3	5	7	1	4	9
4	3	7	8	9	1	5	2	6

214

8	1	5	9	3	7	2	4	6
6	7	2	5	1	4	9	3	8
3	4	9	6	8	2	5	7	1
4	5	6	3	7	9	8	1	2
7	9	8	4	2	1	3	6	5
1	2	3	8	5	6	4	9	7
2	6	4	1	9	8	7	5	3
9	3	7	2	6	5	1	8	4
5	8	1	7	4	3	6	2	9

215

8	9	5	2	4	1	6	7	3
2	4	1	3	7	6	8	5	9
3	6	7	5	9	8	4	1	2
7	5	8	4	2	9	1	3	6
9	3	6	7	1	5	2	4	8
4	1	2	8	6	3	7	9	5
6	8	3	1	5	7	9	2	4
5	7	4	9	8	2	3	6	1
1	2	9	6	3	4	5	8	7

216

2	6	1	4	5	7	9	8	3
5	4	9	8	6	3	7	2	1
3	8	7	2	9	1	5	4	6
7	2	8	3	1	4	6	9	5
6	9	4	5	7	2	3	1	8
1	5	3	9	8	6	4	7	2
8	7	2	6	4	5	1	3	9
4	3	6	1	2	9	8	5	7
9	1	5	7	3	8	2	6	4

217

5	3	8	2	7	1	4	6	9
2	1	6	3	4	9	7	5	8
7	9	4	5	6	8	1	2	3
3	8	1	6	2	4	9	7	5
6	5	9	8	1	7	3	4	2
4	7	2	9	5	3	8	1	6
9	4	5	1	8	2	6	3	7
1	2	3	7	9	6	5	8	4
8	6	7	4	3	5	2	9	1

218

2	9	4	1	3	5	7	6	8
7	1	8	2	4	6	9	5	3
3	5	6	7	8	9	2	1	4
8	7	9	5	1	3	6	4	2
1	3	2	4	6	8	5	9	7
6	4	5	9	7	2	8	3	1
4	8	7	6	5	1	3	2	9
5	2	3	8	9	4	1	7	6
9	6	1	3	2	7	4	8	5

219

3	9	1	7	8	2	5	6	4
4	5	7	9	1	6	8	3	2
8	6	2	5	3	4	7	1	9
7	8	6	2	4	5	3	9	1
9	1	4	3	6	7	2	5	8
5	2	3	8	9	1	4	7	6
2	7	9	6	5	8	1	4	3
6	4	5	1	2	3	9	8	7
1	3	8	4	7	9	6	2	5

220

3	5	8	1	7	6	4	9	2
4	6	1	9	2	3	5	7	8
2	7	9	5	8	4	6	1	3
9	4	2	3	5	8	1	6	7
5	8	7	4	6	1	3	2	9
1	3	6	2	9	7	8	5	4
7	9	3	6	4	5	2	8	1
6	2	4	8	1	9	7	3	5
8	1	5	7	3	2	9	4	6

221

9	3	5	2	7	6	4	8	1
7	2	1	9	8	4	3	5	6
8	6	4	1	3	5	9	7	2
3	1	6	4	9	8	7	2	5
4	7	9	6	5	2	8	1	3
5	8	2	3	1	7	6	4	9
6	9	7	5	4	1	2	3	8
1	4	3	8	2	9	5	6	7
2	5	8	7	6	3	1	9	4

222

2	5	1	7	3	9	8	6	4
9	4	7	6	8	5	3	2	1
3	6	8	2	4	1	9	5	7
7	3	4	9	2	6	1	8	5
5	2	9	8	1	4	6	7	3
8	1	6	3	5	7	2	4	9
6	8	5	4	9	3	7	1	2
4	7	3	1	6	2	5	9	8
1	9	2	5	7	8	4	3	6

223

2	3	9	5	4	6	1	7	8
8	4	7	1	2	9	6	3	5
6	1	5	7	3	8	9	4	2
3	6	4	9	8	5	7	2	1
7	5	1	2	6	4	3	8	9
9	8	2	3	1	7	5	6	4
1	9	3	8	7	2	4	5	6
4	7	8	6	5	1	2	9	3
5	2	6	4	9	3	8	1	7

224

5	2	1	4	7	8	9	6	3
7	3	8	6	2	9	5	4	1
6	4	9	3	5	1	8	2	7
8	7	6	1	9	3	4	5	2
9	5	4	2	8	7	1	3	6
3	1	2	5	6	4	7	8	9
1	8	5	9	3	2	6	7	4
2	9	7	8	4	6	3	1	5
4	6	3	7	1	5	2	9	8

225

5	2	3	9	1	7	8	6	4
7	4	8	2	3	6	9	5	1
9	6	1	5	4	8	3	7	2
3	5	7	6	8	4	2	1	9
6	9	4	3	2	1	5	8	7
8	1	2	7	5	9	4	3	6
1	7	5	8	9	2	6	4	3
4	3	9	1	6	5	7	2	8
2	8	6	4	7	3	1	9	5

226

2	6	3	1	8	9	5	4	7
7	5	1	2	6	4	3	9	8
4	8	9	3	7	5	2	6	1
3	1	4	6	2	7	9	8	5
6	2	8	5	9	1	7	3	4
9	7	5	4	3	8	6	1	2
1	3	7	9	4	2	8	5	6
5	9	2	8	1	6	4	7	3
8	4	6	7	5	3	1	2	9

227

5	8	1	7	4	2	9	6	3
6	9	4	3	5	1	2	7	8
3	7	2	9	6	8	5	1	4
8	4	9	2	1	3	7	5	6
7	1	3	5	8	6	4	2	9
2	6	5	4	9	7	8	3	1
4	3	8	1	7	5	6	9	2
1	5	6	8	2	9	3	4	7
9	2	7	6	3	4	1	8	5

228

6	4	8	7	1	9	5	2	3
5	9	7	3	8	2	1	6	4
3	2	1	4	6	5	9	8	7
4	8	5	2	9	3	7	1	6
2	7	3	1	4	6	8	5	9
1	6	9	8	5	7	4	3	2
9	3	6	5	7	8	2	4	1
8	1	2	9	3	4	6	7	5
7	5	4	6	2	1	3	9	8

229

7	9	6	4	3	2	5	8	1
2	4	3	5	8	1	7	9	6
1	8	5	6	7	9	2	3	4
4	7	9	1	2	5	8	6	3
6	1	8	3	9	7	4	2	5
5	3	2	8	6	4	1	7	9
9	6	1	2	4	8	3	5	7
8	5	7	9	1	3	6	4	2
3	2	4	7	5	6	9	1	8

230

9	1	6	5	8	4	7	3	2
5	2	4	7	1	3	6	8	9
7	8	3	9	6	2	5	1	4
8	5	9	2	4	7	1	6	3
3	6	1	8	5	9	2	4	7
4	7	2	6	3	1	9	5	8
2	3	8	1	9	6	4	7	5
6	4	7	3	2	5	8	9	1
1	9	5	4	7	8	3	2	6

231

8	2	7	1	3	6	9	5	4
9	4	5	7	8	2	3	6	1
1	6	3	4	9	5	7	2	8
6	9	1	2	5	4	8	3	7
4	7	2	3	6	8	1	9	5
3	5	8	9	1	7	2	4	6
5	1	6	8	2	9	4	7	3
2	8	4	6	7	3	5	1	9
7	3	9	5	4	1	6	8	2

232

2	8	9	5	3	1	6	4	7
3	7	6	9	4	8	1	5	2
1	5	4	6	7	2	9	8	3
5	6	8	4	2	9	7	3	1
7	1	3	8	5	6	4	2	9
9	4	2	3	1	7	5	6	8
6	3	1	2	9	4	8	7	5
4	2	7	1	8	5	3	9	6
8	9	5	7	6	3	2	1	4

233

3	2	5	4	6	7	8	1	9
1	9	7	2	8	3	4	6	5
4	8	6	9	1	5	7	2	3
5	1	8	6	9	4	2	3	7
2	6	3	7	5	8	9	4	1
9	7	4	1	3	2	6	5	8
7	4	9	5	2	1	3	8	6
8	5	2	3	7	6	1	9	4
6	3	1	8	4	9	5	7	2

234

1	5	3	2	7	4	9	6	8
4	2	7	8	9	6	5	3	1
8	9	6	5	1	3	4	2	7
7	4	9	3	2	1	8	5	6
3	1	2	6	8	5	7	9	4
5	6	8	9	4	7	2	1	3
2	7	4	1	3	9	6	8	5
6	8	1	4	5	2	3	7	9
9	3	5	7	6	8	1	4	2

235

5	4	6	9	3	1	8	7	2
8	7	1	5	6	2	3	4	9
2	3	9	7	8	4	5	6	1
1	6	4	2	9	5	7	8	3
3	8	2	6	1	7	9	5	4
9	5	7	3	4	8	2	1	6
7	2	3	1	5	6	4	9	8
6	9	8	4	7	3	1	2	5
4	1	5	8	2	9	6	3	7

236

8	7	9	5	4	3	2	6	1
6	2	5	8	9	1	7	3	4
4	1	3	7	2	6	5	9	8
9	6	7	2	5	4	8	1	3
1	4	2	6	3	8	9	5	7
3	5	8	1	7	9	4	2	6
7	8	6	9	1	5	3	4	2
2	9	4	3	6	7	1	8	5
5	3	1	4	8	2	6	7	9

237

1	4	8	6	7	3	5	2	9
2	9	3	5	1	8	4	7	6
7	5	6	4	2	9	3	1	8
9	6	4	2	5	1	8	3	7
3	2	1	7	8	6	9	4	5
5	8	7	3	9	4	1	6	2
8	3	2	9	4	7	6	5	1
6	1	5	8	3	2	7	9	4
4	7	9	1	6	5	2	8	3

238

3	1	5	4	2	8	7	6	9
7	2	8	9	3	6	4	1	5
4	9	6	7	5	1	8	2	3
9	7	3	6	8	5	2	4	1
5	4	1	2	7	9	3	8	6
6	8	2	3	1	4	9	5	7
8	3	9	1	6	2	5	7	4
2	6	4	5	9	7	1	3	8
1	5	7	8	4	3	6	9	2

239

5	7	8	9	1	4	3	2	6
4	2	3	5	8	6	1	9	7
1	6	9	3	2	7	4	8	5
7	1	6	8	4	5	9	3	2
9	3	4	1	6	2	5	7	8
8	5	2	7	9	3	6	1	4
2	9	5	4	3	8	7	6	1
3	8	7	6	5	1	2	4	9
6	4	1	2	7	9	8	5	3

240

8	1	4	7	9	3	5	2	6
3	6	5	1	4	2	9	7	8
9	2	7	8	6	5	1	3	4
2	7	3	5	1	8	4	6	9
5	8	6	9	2	4	7	1	3
4	9	1	3	7	6	2	8	5
7	3	9	4	8	1	6	5	2
1	5	2	6	3	9	8	4	7
6	4	8	2	5	7	3	9	1

241

9	8	4	5	3	2	1	6	7
1	6	2	9	8	7	3	4	5
3	7	5	1	6	4	9	2	8
5	1	6	2	7	3	4	8	9
8	9	7	4	5	6	2	3	1
4	2	3	8	1	9	5	7	6
6	4	1	3	9	8	7	5	2
2	5	8	7	4	1	6	9	3
7	3	9	6	2	5	8	1	4

242

8	5	9	1	6	2	3	7	4
7	2	4	3	5	8	1	6	9
3	6	1	7	4	9	2	5	8
1	8	7	4	9	5	6	3	2
6	9	5	2	7	3	8	4	1
4	3	2	6	8	1	7	9	5
9	7	8	5	1	6	4	2	3
2	1	6	9	3	4	5	8	7
5	4	3	8	2	7	9	1	6

243

7	5	1	9	2	4	8	6	3
8	2	6	3	1	5	4	7	9
9	4	3	7	8	6	1	5	2
6	7	9	1	4	8	3	2	5
3	8	4	5	9	2	6	1	7
2	1	5	6	7	3	9	4	8
5	9	2	4	3	1	7	8	6
1	3	8	2	6	7	5	9	4
4	6	7	8	5	9	2	3	1

244

4	9	8	5	3	2	1	7	6
1	6	3	7	9	8	2	5	4
2	5	7	4	6	1	9	8	3
9	2	4	1	5	7	6	3	8
8	1	5	3	2	6	4	9	7
3	7	6	8	4	9	5	2	1
7	4	9	6	8	5	3	1	2
6	8	2	9	1	3	7	4	5
5	3	1	2	7	4	8	6	9

245

8	3	4	1	2	6	7	9	5
2	5	1	3	7	9	8	4	6
9	6	7	4	8	5	2	3	1
3	9	5	2	1	4	6	8	7
1	4	2	8	6	7	3	5	9
7	8	6	5	9	3	1	2	4
4	7	8	9	3	1	5	6	2
6	2	9	7	5	8	4	1	3
5	1	3	6	4	2	9	7	8

246

1	5	3	7	8	2	6	9	4
9	8	7	3	6	4	5	2	1
4	2	6	9	5	1	8	3	7
8	7	1	2	3	5	4	6	9
6	9	2	4	1	7	3	8	5
3	4	5	8	9	6	7	1	2
7	3	9	1	4	8	2	5	6
5	1	4	6	2	3	9	7	8
2	6	8	5	7	9	1	4	3

247

9	4	8	7	1	3	5	2	6
3	5	7	2	6	9	4	8	1
1	2	6	4	5	8	3	7	9
2	3	4	8	9	1	7	6	5
6	1	5	3	7	4	8	9	2
7	8	9	5	2	6	1	4	3
5	7	3	9	8	2	6	1	4
4	6	2	1	3	7	9	5	8
8	9	1	6	4	5	2	3	7

248

5	7	9	2	4	8	6	3	1
8	3	2	7	6	1	5	4	9
6	4	1	3	9	5	2	8	7
1	9	4	5	3	7	8	2	6
2	8	5	6	1	4	7	9	3
7	6	3	8	2	9	1	5	4
9	5	7	4	8	6	3	1	2
4	2	8	1	7	3	9	6	5
3	1	6	9	5	2	4	7	8

249

4	9	8	7	5	6	3	1	2
7	1	5	2	4	3	8	6	9
6	3	2	9	1	8	4	5	7
9	5	3	8	6	2	7	4	1
8	2	7	4	9	1	6	3	5
1	4	6	3	7	5	2	9	8
5	8	9	6	3	7	1	2	4
3	7	4	1	2	9	5	8	6
2	6	1	5	8	4	9	7	3

250

2	9	3	8	7	6	1	4	5
7	8	5	1	4	3	6	2	9
6	4	1	5	9	2	3	8	7
3	1	7	9	5	4	2	6	8
4	5	8	2	6	1	9	7	3
9	6	2	7	3	8	5	1	4
1	7	9	4	2	5	8	3	6
8	3	4	6	1	9	7	5	2
5	2	6	3	8	7	4	9	1

251

3	4	5	8	6	2	7	9	1
2	9	1	4	7	5	3	6	8
6	8	7	1	9	3	4	2	5
9	5	3	2	1	7	8	4	6
7	1	8	6	4	9	5	3	2
4	6	2	5	3	8	1	7	9
1	3	6	9	5	4	2	8	7
8	7	9	3	2	1	6	5	4
5	2	4	7	8	6	9	1	3

252

8	9	2	4	1	3	7	5	6
7	4	1	8	6	5	2	3	9
3	5	6	7	9	2	1	8	4
2	7	9	5	8	1	6	4	3
1	3	8	9	4	6	5	2	7
5	6	4	3	2	7	9	1	8
9	2	3	6	5	4	8	7	1
4	8	5	1	7	9	3	6	2
6	1	7	2	3	8	4	9	5

253

8	6	7	4	9	1	5	3	2
5	9	1	2	3	6	7	4	8
2	4	3	5	8	7	9	6	1
6	3	2	8	5	4	1	9	7
4	5	8	1	7	9	6	2	3
7	1	9	6	2	3	4	8	5
3	8	6	7	4	5	2	1	9
9	7	4	3	1	2	8	5	6
1	2	5	9	6	8	3	7	4

254

8	2	4	9	3	6	7	1	5
1	5	3	4	7	2	8	6	9
7	6	9	8	1	5	3	4	2
9	4	5	3	2	8	1	7	6
2	1	8	6	5	7	9	3	4
3	7	6	1	9	4	2	5	8
6	3	2	5	8	1	4	9	7
4	9	7	2	6	3	5	8	1
5	8	1	7	4	9	6	2	3

255

9	4	5	3	1	8	6	2	7
1	3	7	2	9	6	4	5	8
2	8	6	7	4	5	3	1	9
4	1	9	8	6	2	5	7	3
5	6	3	9	7	1	8	4	2
8	7	2	4	5	3	9	6	1
3	9	4	5	2	7	1	8	6
6	2	8	1	3	4	7	9	5
7	5	1	6	8	9	2	3	4

256

9	2	3	8	4	5	7	6	1
1	8	4	6	3	7	9	5	2
5	7	6	9	1	2	8	4	3
2	5	8	3	9	4	1	7	6
4	1	7	5	8	6	2	3	9
6	3	9	7	2	1	4	8	5
8	6	2	4	5	9	3	1	7
3	9	5	1	7	8	6	2	4
7	4	1	2	6	3	5	9	8

257

7	1	2	8	3	9	6	4	5
6	5	9	7	4	1	8	2	3
8	3	4	6	2	5	1	9	7
5	8	3	9	6	4	2	7	1
4	2	1	3	5	7	9	6	8
9	6	7	1	8	2	3	5	4
2	4	6	5	1	8	7	3	9
1	9	5	2	7	3	4	8	6
3	7	8	4	9	6	5	1	2

258

5	1	8	9	7	2	3	4	6
6	3	9	4	8	1	2	7	5
4	7	2	3	5	6	1	8	9
2	6	1	5	4	8	7	9	3
8	9	3	1	6	7	4	5	2
7	5	4	2	3	9	8	6	1
3	2	5	7	9	4	6	1	8
1	8	7	6	2	5	9	3	4
9	4	6	8	1	3	5	2	7

259

3	4	6	1	2	5	8	9	7
9	8	7	4	6	3	1	5	2
1	5	2	9	8	7	6	3	4
4	2	3	5	1	9	7	6	8
6	1	5	8	7	4	9	2	3
8	7	9	6	3	2	4	1	5
5	3	1	7	4	6	2	8	9
7	9	8	2	5	1	3	4	6
2	6	4	3	9	8	5	7	1

260

3	8	6	2	9	4	1	7	5
4	1	9	5	7	6	8	3	2
7	5	2	8	3	1	9	4	6
9	2	1	6	4	7	3	5	8
5	4	8	3	1	2	7	6	9
6	7	3	9	8	5	2	1	4
2	9	4	7	5	3	6	8	1
1	6	7	4	2	8	5	9	3
8	3	5	1	6	9	4	2	7

261

2	5	8	7	4	1	3	9	6
6	3	4	2	8	9	5	1	7
7	9	1	3	5	6	8	4	2
5	7	6	9	3	4	1	2	8
1	8	2	5	6	7	9	3	4
3	4	9	1	2	8	6	7	5
4	1	3	6	7	5	2	8	9
9	6	7	8	1	2	4	5	3
8	2	5	4	9	3	7	6	1

262

8	1	5	3	2	4	7	6	9
3	2	4	6	7	9	5	8	1
6	7	9	5	8	1	4	2	3
1	5	3	9	4	8	2	7	6
7	8	6	1	3	2	9	5	4
4	9	2	7	6	5	1	3	8
9	6	7	2	1	3	8	4	5
5	3	8	4	9	7	6	1	2
2	4	1	8	5	6	3	9	7

263

2	6	9	5	8	1	7	4	3
7	4	3	2	9	6	1	8	5
1	8	5	7	4	3	2	6	9
8	1	2	3	7	5	6	9	4
6	9	7	8	2	4	5	3	1
3	5	4	6	1	9	8	2	7
4	3	8	1	6	7	9	5	2
9	7	6	4	5	2	3	1	8
5	2	1	9	3	8	4	7	6

264

9	7	6	3	2	4	1	5	8
4	8	2	5	1	9	3	7	6
3	1	5	7	8	6	9	2	4
5	2	4	8	3	1	6	9	7
7	6	8	4	9	2	5	1	3
1	9	3	6	5	7	8	4	2
8	4	7	9	6	5	2	3	1
6	5	1	2	4	3	7	8	9
2	3	9	1	7	8	4	6	5

265

7	1	9	5	3	6	8	2	4
3	8	4	2	1	9	7	6	5
2	6	5	8	7	4	3	1	9
9	7	2	1	4	5	6	8	3
4	3	6	7	2	8	9	5	1
1	5	8	6	9	3	2	4	7
8	9	1	4	6	7	5	3	2
6	2	7	3	5	1	4	9	8
5	4	3	9	8	2	1	7	6

266

9	7	5	2	4	3	1	8	6
1	3	6	5	8	9	2	4	7
4	8	2	6	7	1	5	3	9
2	6	7	9	5	4	8	1	3
8	1	4	3	2	7	6	9	5
5	9	3	1	6	8	7	2	4
7	4	1	8	3	5	9	6	2
6	5	9	4	1	2	3	7	8
3	2	8	7	9	6	4	5	1

267

8	2	1	9	6	5	4	7	3
9	7	3	8	1	4	5	2	6
5	6	4	2	3	7	1	9	8
6	4	9	7	8	3	2	5	1
1	8	7	5	2	6	9	3	4
3	5	2	1	4	9	8	6	7
2	3	5	4	7	8	6	1	9
4	1	6	3	9	2	7	8	5
7	9	8	6	5	1	3	4	2

268

9	7	4	3	8	2	5	6	1
8	5	1	7	6	4	2	9	3
3	6	2	1	5	9	4	8	7
2	1	7	8	9	5	3	4	6
6	9	3	4	7	1	8	5	2
5	4	8	2	3	6	1	7	9
4	8	9	6	1	3	7	2	5
7	3	6	5	2	8	9	1	4
1	2	5	9	4	7	6	3	8

269

2	1	3	4	6	5	8	9	7
4	6	5	9	7	8	2	3	1
7	9	8	1	2	3	6	5	4
3	4	2	7	8	9	1	6	5
6	5	9	2	1	4	3	7	8
1	8	7	3	5	6	4	2	9
8	2	1	5	3	7	9	4	6
9	7	6	8	4	2	5	1	3
5	3	4	6	9	1	7	8	2

270

5	7	9	4	2	3	6	8	1
2	8	4	7	1	6	9	3	5
3	6	1	9	5	8	7	2	4
4	9	2	3	6	5	1	7	8
7	1	3	8	9	2	5	4	6
6	5	8	1	7	4	3	9	2
9	2	7	5	4	1	8	6	3
1	3	6	2	8	9	4	5	7
8	4	5	6	3	7	2	1	9

271

3	5	1	4	8	9	7	6	2
9	8	2	6	7	5	3	1	4
7	4	6	1	3	2	8	9	5
4	3	9	2	6	7	1	5	8
5	1	8	3	9	4	2	7	6
2	6	7	8	5	1	4	3	9
1	9	5	7	4	8	6	2	3
8	7	3	5	2	6	9	4	1
6	2	4	9	1	3	5	8	7

272

8	3	5	1	7	6	2	9	4
7	4	1	9	2	8	3	5	6
6	2	9	5	4	3	8	7	1
9	6	7	8	1	2	4	3	5
5	1	2	3	9	4	7	6	8
4	8	3	7	6	5	1	2	9
3	7	8	6	5	1	9	4	2
2	9	6	4	8	7	5	1	3
1	5	4	2	3	9	6	8	7

273

5	4	7	9	8	6	2	3	1
8	6	2	7	3	1	5	9	4
1	9	3	5	4	2	6	7	8
4	2	5	3	9	7	1	8	6
9	3	8	1	6	4	7	2	5
7	1	6	8	2	5	9	4	3
3	8	1	2	5	9	4	6	7
6	5	9	4	7	8	3	1	2
2	7	4	6	1	3	8	5	9

274

8	5	7	4	2	3	1	9	6
3	1	2	6	7	9	4	8	5
4	6	9	1	8	5	2	7	3
2	3	8	9	4	6	7	5	1
1	4	6	8	5	7	3	2	9
7	9	5	3	1	2	8	6	4
5	7	4	2	6	1	9	3	8
6	8	3	7	9	4	5	1	2
9	2	1	5	3	8	6	4	7

275

2	6	5	3	9	7	4	8	1
1	3	4	6	2	8	9	5	7
9	7	8	4	5	1	3	6	2
8	5	1	2	7	4	6	9	3
6	4	3	9	1	5	2	7	8
7	2	9	8	3	6	1	4	5
4	1	6	5	8	3	7	2	9
5	9	7	1	4	2	8	3	6
3	8	2	7	6	9	5	1	4

276

1	5	4	6	8	2	9	7	3
2	8	9	3	4	7	5	1	6
6	7	3	1	5	9	8	4	2
3	6	7	9	1	4	2	8	5
8	9	5	7	2	6	4	3	1
4	2	1	5	3	8	7	6	9
7	1	2	4	6	5	3	9	8
5	4	6	8	9	3	1	2	7
9	3	8	2	7	1	6	5	4

277

6	3	7	2	5	8	9	4	1
4	8	2	1	6	9	3	5	7
9	5	1	7	3	4	6	8	2
1	9	3	6	7	5	8	2	4
7	4	6	9	8	2	1	3	5
5	2	8	4	1	3	7	6	9
2	6	5	8	9	1	4	7	3
3	7	9	5	4	6	2	1	8
8	1	4	3	2	7	5	9	6

278

1	4	9	7	6	3	2	5	8
5	2	3	8	9	1	6	4	7
6	8	7	2	5	4	3	9	1
2	1	4	6	8	5	7	3	9
9	7	5	1	3	2	8	6	4
8	3	6	9	4	7	1	2	5
4	9	1	3	7	6	5	8	2
7	6	8	5	2	9	4	1	3
3	5	2	4	1	8	9	7	6

279

5	6	9	2	7	3	4	1	8
7	2	1	9	8	4	5	3	6
8	3	4	6	5	1	7	9	2
3	8	7	5	4	9	6	2	1
6	1	5	3	2	8	9	4	7
4	9	2	7	1	6	8	5	3
9	7	8	4	3	2	1	6	5
1	4	3	8	6	5	2	7	9
2	5	6	1	9	7	3	8	4

280

6	7	5	4	2	9	1	3	8
9	1	4	3	7	8	2	6	5
8	3	2	6	5	1	7	9	4
2	5	8	1	4	3	6	7	9
7	6	9	5	8	2	3	4	1
3	4	1	7	9	6	5	8	2
1	8	7	9	6	5	4	2	3
5	2	6	8	3	4	9	1	7
4	9	3	2	1	7	8	5	6

281

8	4	1	2	6	9	3	5	7
9	6	2	5	7	3	8	1	4
3	5	7	8	4	1	2	6	9
7	3	8	4	1	2	5	9	6
5	1	6	3	9	8	7	4	2
2	9	4	6	5	7	1	3	8
4	7	5	1	2	6	9	8	3
1	2	3	9	8	4	6	7	5
6	8	9	7	3	5	4	2	1

282

5	7	1	3	4	9	8	6	2
9	4	2	1	6	8	7	3	5
8	3	6	5	7	2	1	4	9
7	8	3	2	5	1	4	9	6
1	6	5	9	3	4	2	8	7
2	9	4	6	8	7	3	5	1
3	5	7	4	1	6	9	2	8
4	2	8	7	9	5	6	1	3
6	1	9	8	2	3	5	7	4

283

8	5	9	6	3	4	1	7	2
1	3	4	9	7	2	6	8	5
7	2	6	1	5	8	4	3	9
9	8	3	5	1	6	7	2	4
5	6	7	4	2	9	3	1	8
2	4	1	7	8	3	9	5	6
4	7	2	3	6	5	8	9	1
3	9	8	2	4	1	5	6	7
6	1	5	8	9	7	2	4	3

284

1	3	7	2	4	6	5	9	8
8	4	2	9	7	5	1	6	3
6	5	9	1	3	8	7	2	4
3	6	5	8	2	1	4	7	9
4	7	1	6	9	3	2	8	5
9	2	8	4	5	7	6	3	1
2	8	6	5	1	9	3	4	7
7	1	4	3	8	2	9	5	6
5	9	3	7	6	4	8	1	2

285

9	6	4	3	7	8	5	2	1
3	1	2	9	4	5	8	7	6
7	5	8	1	2	6	4	9	3
5	7	1	6	9	4	3	8	2
4	2	3	5	8	1	7	6	9
8	9	6	2	3	7	1	5	4
6	3	7	8	1	2	9	4	5
2	8	9	4	5	3	6	1	7
1	4	5	7	6	9	2	3	8

286

7	4	1	5	8	9	2	6	3
2	8	3	7	4	6	9	1	5
5	9	6	1	2	3	7	4	8
4	1	7	3	9	5	6	8	2
9	3	5	2	6	8	1	7	4
8	6	2	4	7	1	3	5	9
1	2	9	6	5	4	8	3	7
3	5	8	9	1	7	4	2	6
6	7	4	8	3	2	5	9	1

287

1	8	4	7	3	6	5	2	9
9	5	2	8	4	1	7	6	3
7	3	6	9	5	2	4	1	8
3	6	8	2	9	7	1	5	4
4	9	1	5	6	8	2	3	7
5	2	7	4	1	3	8	9	6
8	1	3	6	7	5	9	4	2
2	4	5	3	8	9	6	7	1
6	7	9	1	2	4	3	8	5

288

3	4	8	2	5	6	9	7	1
6	7	9	4	3	1	2	8	5
2	1	5	8	7	9	3	6	4
1	5	3	6	2	4	8	9	7
9	8	7	3	1	5	6	4	2
4	2	6	7	9	8	5	1	3
8	3	2	1	6	7	4	5	9
7	9	4	5	8	2	1	3	6
5	6	1	9	4	3	7	2	8

289

6	2	8	5	9	1	3	4	7
5	7	9	4	3	8	6	1	2
3	1	4	2	7	6	9	8	5
8	4	1	9	2	3	5	7	6
2	3	7	6	5	4	8	9	1
9	5	6	1	8	7	4	2	3
4	6	5	8	1	2	7	3	9
1	8	3	7	6	9	2	5	4
7	9	2	3	4	5	1	6	8

290

1	9	2	3	5	4	8	6	7
3	5	8	1	6	7	9	4	2
4	6	7	9	8	2	1	3	5
2	1	6	8	3	5	4	7	9
9	4	5	7	2	6	3	1	8
7	8	3	4	1	9	2	5	6
8	7	9	6	4	1	5	2	3
5	3	1	2	7	8	6	9	4
6	2	4	5	9	3	7	8	1

291

2	5	1	9	8	4	6	7	3
4	9	8	3	7	6	2	1	5
6	3	7	1	2	5	8	4	9
7	4	5	8	3	2	9	6	1
9	8	2	5	6	1	7	3	4
3	1	6	4	9	7	5	2	8
8	6	4	2	5	3	1	9	7
5	7	3	6	1	9	4	8	2
1	2	9	7	4	8	3	5	6

292

9	7	8	1	6	2	3	5	4
3	1	5	4	9	7	8	6	2
6	2	4	8	5	3	1	7	9
2	4	7	5	8	6	9	3	1
1	8	3	9	7	4	5	2	6
5	9	6	2	3	1	7	4	8
8	5	2	7	4	9	6	1	3
4	3	9	6	1	5	2	8	7
7	6	1	3	2	8	4	9	5

293

5	6	3	1	9	2	8	7	4
8	7	4	3	5	6	2	1	9
1	2	9	8	7	4	6	5	3
3	9	5	7	1	8	4	6	2
2	4	8	5	6	9	7	3	1
6	1	7	2	4	3	9	8	5
4	5	1	6	2	7	3	9	8
7	3	2	9	8	5	1	4	6
9	8	6	4	3	1	5	2	7

294

1	8	5	3	6	7	9	2	4
2	6	9	5	4	1	7	3	8
4	7	3	2	8	9	1	6	5
3	5	7	6	9	4	8	1	2
9	4	2	1	3	8	5	7	6
6	1	8	7	5	2	3	4	9
5	9	1	4	2	3	6	8	7
8	3	4	9	7	6	2	5	1
7	2	6	8	1	5	4	9	3

295

7	6	5	1	4	9	3	8	2
4	1	8	2	5	3	9	7	6
2	3	9	7	6	8	1	5	4
9	7	6	5	2	1	4	3	8
1	8	2	6	3	4	7	9	5
5	4	3	9	8	7	6	2	1
8	9	1	4	7	5	2	6	3
6	5	4	3	9	2	8	1	7
3	2	7	8	1	6	5	4	9

296

5	4	8	7	6	9	3	1	2
2	3	6	8	5	1	7	9	4
7	1	9	4	2	3	6	8	5
1	5	7	2	8	4	9	6	3
8	9	2	3	7	6	4	5	1
3	6	4	9	1	5	8	2	7
4	8	5	6	3	2	1	7	9
9	7	1	5	4	8	2	3	6
6	2	3	1	9	7	5	4	8

297

2	8	3	4	6	5	7	9	1
4	6	1	9	7	3	8	5	2
7	9	5	2	8	1	3	4	6
3	1	9	6	2	8	5	7	4
8	7	2	3	5	4	1	6	9
5	4	6	1	9	7	2	8	3
1	5	4	8	3	6	9	2	7
9	3	8	7	4	2	6	1	5
6	2	7	5	1	9	4	3	8

298

1	9	4	7	6	2	3	8	5
8	3	7	4	5	1	6	2	9
6	2	5	9	8	3	4	1	7
5	4	9	2	7	6	8	3	1
7	6	1	5	3	8	2	9	4
2	8	3	1	4	9	7	5	6
3	5	6	8	9	4	1	7	2
4	7	2	3	1	5	9	6	8
9	1	8	6	2	7	5	4	3

299

4	1	9	5	2	3	6	7	8
2	7	6	9	1	8	5	4	3
3	5	8	6	4	7	2	9	1
9	4	1	3	5	6	8	2	7
6	2	7	1	8	4	3	5	9
8	3	5	7	9	2	1	6	4
1	8	4	2	6	9	7	3	5
5	6	3	4	7	1	9	8	2
7	9	2	8	3	5	4	1	6

300

6	2	5	7	4	3	1	8	9
7	4	3	8	1	9	5	6	2
8	1	9	6	5	2	7	3	4
9	7	2	1	3	8	4	5	6
5	3	1	4	9	6	8	2	7
4	6	8	2	7	5	3	9	1
3	8	4	9	2	7	6	1	5
1	9	6	5	8	4	2	7	3
2	5	7	3	6	1	9	4	8